D0364331

A PASSION FOR PLANTS

A PASSION FOR PLANTS

Behind the scenes at the
Royal Horticultural
Society

CAROLYN FRY

contents

foreword
by Alan Titchmarsh MBE VMH

There are very few gardens peopled with quite so many passionate gardeners as those that are part of the Royal Horticultural Society. Among them is the RHS garden at Wisley, which I've been going to regularly for forty years now, either to make television programmes, to meet some of the staff – be they experts in pests and diseases, alpines or rhododendrons – or simply for pleasure. It never fails to inspire me, and neither do the members of staff, because, as centres of excellence go, Wisley takes some beating. Over the years the Society has grown in size and influence. It now has gardens in Britain at all four points of the compass – at Harlow Carr in Yorkshire, Hyde Hall in Essex, Rosemoor in Devon and Wisley in Surrey – and its shows fill the gardening and social calendar. But back on its home turf the craft of gardening is still of prime importance.

When I was a student at Kew Gardens there was a healthy rivalry with 'the other place', as Wisley was known. We staged debates, swapped information and even traded good-natured insults. My loyalty to Kew remains, but so does my affection and respect for the RHS and its people.

Knowledge, they say, is power, but at the Royal Horticultural Society they share their knowledge with unstinting generosity, empowering their members and encouraging their interest in things that grow. If you are a member of the RHS – and anyone can be – you have access to a rich vein of expertise that is freely dispensed. Give them a problem and terrier-like they will get to the bottom of it. From the Director-General at the top of the Society's tree to the humblest gardener down, literally, at grass-roots level, each and every member of the RHS staff knows that theirs is a special sort of job. And that makes them exceptional people. This book is a tribute to their efforts and their passion, and a worthy memento of some remarkable gardens.

introduction
by Inga Grimsey, RHS Director-General

Every spring and summer, the Royal Horticultural Society attracts over 400,000 members of the public to its annual Flower Shows and receives up to a million visitors to its four gardens. Yet this is just the tip of the iceberg of the RHS and its work. Ever since it was established in 1804, the Royal Horticultural Society has been at the forefront of horticultural excellence, encouraging people of all ages and from all walks of life to share a passion for plants and inspiring anyone with an interest in gardening. In recognition of this, *A Passion for Plants* not only charts the Society's rich and varied history but also reveals that, while remaining close to its charitable roots, the RHS as an organization is very much of the twenty-first century.

Unearthing the various strands of the RHS's less well-known activities, *A Passion for Plants* explores the vital outreach and educational programmes that aim not only to enthuse and educate the gardeners of the future but also, in a time of social change, give children, especially, an understanding of how things grow, the impact of the environment on plants and where food comes from. It also details the complex work carried out by the Trials and Science departments, which is the basis for so much of our advice, knowledge and garden practice. And it profiles the Royal Horticultural Society's own gardens – Harlow Carr, Hyde Hall, Rosemoor and Wisley – which are taking a fundamental lead in embracing the responsibility that we all have as gardeners to garden sustainably, with the environment and changing climate in mind. These topics highlight the important areas of development for the RHS in the next few years: connecting with an increasing number of gardeners through membership and support, engaging with and supplying activities and education for more children and young people and leading gardeners in the challenges of environmental issues, of climate change in particular.

As a relative newcomer to the Royal Horticultural Society, I am as fascinated as any member of the public by the many layers that make up such a respected institution. But, more important, I am delighted that *A Passion for Plants* celebrates the personalities behind the scenes of the Society, the people whose unstinting dedication and passion for gardening, horticulture and the environment make it happen.

CHAPTER 1
the green revolution

Sustainability has become the buzzword for twenty-first century living. Having squandered the Earth's bounty of resources for centuries, the consequences of our actions are coming back to haunt us. By destroying finely tuned ecosystems in rainforests, deserts, oceans and rivers, we have threatened thousands of plants and animals with extinction and irrevocably altered natural systems on which we rely for food and water. And by pumping greenhouse gases into the atmosphere as a result of burning fossil fuels to heat our homes and power our cars we have now begun to alter the world's climate. As a WWF report recently pointed out, if we continue living in this wasteful way, we shall need three planets to support us.

Gardeners and botanists have rather poor past records when it comes to looking after the environment. In the heyday of plant collecting, explorers thought nothing of felling an entire tree in order to snatch a single precious orchid from its crown. And commercial transfers of plants during colonial times had disastrous consequences for the indigenous flora of far-flung countries. More recently, chemicals have become an easy remedy for modern gardeners seeking to eradicate unwanted plants and bugs. And peat remains a favourite potting medium, despite being sourced from fragile, non-renewable bogs that release greenhouse gases into the atmosphere when destroyed.

The new green revolution, however, offers an opportunity for gardeners to make amends. The 1 million ha (2½ million acres) of gardens in the UK form an area bigger than all the nature reserves and parks put together. By reducing the use of pesticides, encouraging biodiversity by installing bird, bee and bat boxes, cutting waste and the need to use peat by composting vegetable peelings and garden vegetation, and, as climate change takes hold, using plants that will thrive in a drier climate, gardeners can have a positive influence on the environment and set a leading example for how we can all live more sustainably.

Work with nature

'Inherently, gardeners are working with nature so they are the original "greens",' says Jill Cherry, the Royal Horticultural Society's director of Gardens and Estates. 'However, through the twentieth century, they have been given a lot of tools to use to perfect their gardens that in today's world are not

OPPOSITE *Naturalistic gardening can have a positive impact on the environment*

considered to be very environmentally friendly. The RHS is very well positioned, given our relationship with the UK's gardeners, to make sure we are gardening as sustainably as we can and then to share what we've learnt with others. A lot of the time that means practising some incredibly old truisms. If you are a good gardener, you are working with the right plant for the right place. We need to step back and say, "My garden presents this kind of challenge and opportunity," and then decide, from the broad palette of plants we have access to, what would be the best to grow with the minimum of peat, fertilizer, pesticides and water. We forget that in our enthusiasm for trying to grow something we've fallen in love with.'

A major challenge facing gardeners today is the uncertainty posed by climate change. The ten warmest years recorded globally have all occurred during the last 12 years. The Central England Temperature (CET) record is the oldest continuous dataset for temperature anywhere in the world. Its measurements rank the UK's hottest ten years as 2006, 1999, 1990, 1949,

2002, 1997, 1995, 2003, 1989 and 2004. In 2006, the average temperature was the highest recorded in 347 years of CET measurements, at 1.37°C above average. If the temperature rise continues, as climate scientists predict it will, the coming years will see gardeners facing prolonged droughts and floods, hose-pipe bans and previously unknown garden pests and diseases. 'Across all our gardens we have noticed that there are distinct and very real climatic changes going on,' says Jill.

The RHS's most westerly garden, Rosemoor, in Devon, enveloped by the densely wooded valley of the River Torridge, has, in particular, been experiencing the early effects of climate change. Historically, Rosemoor's frost-prone, valley-bottom microclimate constrained the range of plants that would grow there. When Christopher Bailes took on the job of curator in 1988, spring frosts, which often arrived when new growth was at its most vulnerable, were a key factor in limiting his choice of plants. During his first decade in the job, the garden experienced frosts in April and May that were severe enough to strip leaves from trees over 10 m (30 feet) tall and affect the flowering of mature oaks. Rosemoor's former owner Lady Anne Berry told Christopher he could forget any notions of growing the tender plants characteristic of West Country gardens, as she had tried and been beaten by the capricious microclimate.

'Across all our gardens we have noticed that there are distinct and very real climatic changes going on.'

Christopher was surprised to find, however, that some experiments he tried, such as growing tree ferns and the Mediterranean fan palm (*Chamaerops*) were successful. In the past eight or so years, he has succeeded in growing numerous previously tender plants, including *Geranium maderense*, *Lomatia*, *Tetrapanax*, a range of acacias and the Chilean bellflower, *Lapageria*. Whereas once he would lift large plants of *Musa basjoo*, the Japanese hardy banana, into dustbins for overwintering in polytunnels, he now simply swathes the base in dry bracken fronds for insulation and leaves them *in situ*. Today's milder winters mean that some plants not able to tolerate late frosts are now hardy. 'When Lady Anne comes back here, and I take her around the garden, she's amazed at what we can grow that she previously couldn't,' he says.

OPPOSITE *The range of plants that thrive at Rosemoor is expanding, thanks to climate change*

Water wisely

With a continued warming trend, water use is likely to become a critical issue for gardeners. Viewed from space our blue, watery planet looks as if it has a never-ending supply of this life-giving liquid, but only 3 per cent of it is not salty. Two-thirds of our fresh water is locked up in ice caps and glaciers. Of the remaining 1 per cent, a fifth is in remote, inaccessible areas, and a good deal of the rest arrives when it is least wanted, as monsoonal deluges and floods. The result is that humans are able to exploit only 0.08 per cent of all the world's water. In the UK, reservoirs are frequently running low in dry years. In early 2007, DEFRA announced it was to review hose-pipe ban legislation, saying: 'We cannot ignore the fact that the frequency of droughts may increase in future, and we must be ready for that possibility.'

ABOVE *The Dry Garden at Hyde Hall contains plants that are adapted for drier environments*

The RHS Garden at Hyde Hall is ideally situated to demonstrate plants likely to thrive in a warmer Britain. Located close to the driest place in the UK, St Osyth in Essex, it receives less rainfall annually than Jerusalem or Beirut. In 2001, the then curator, Matthew Wilson, now Curator and Head of Site at the RHS's most northerly garden, Harlow Carr in Yorkshire, decided to capitalize on the garden's natural environment and, at the same time, demonstrate to gardeners how they could cut water use by choosing plants adapted for drier environments. 'The driving force for it was the fact that Essex is one of the driest counties in the UK,' he says. 'We have an east–west climatic divide in the UK, with the west being wetter and the east being drier. We wanted to create a planting that looked a little like a rocky Mediterranean hillside and that demonstrated the range of plants you can grow without any irrigation at all.'

Matthew's team constructed the Dry Garden on a sloping 1600-sq-m (2000-sq-yard) site using large boulders of igneous rock and a stone mulch to create a rocky environment similar to the natural habitat of many of the plants. Good drainage is essential for drought-tolerant plants, so they covered the rubble-filled subsoil with a gritty top layer. The team selected plants that could tolerate drought, exposure and high light levels. Many of them carry the RHS Award of Garden Merit (for more about this, see page 144). The garden's south-facing aspect means that the plants get plenty of sun, and individual rocks help to create microclimates for more tender plants. 'The Dry Garden is full of "camel" plants that have adapted to survive in hot, dry conditions such as you get in the Mediterranean basin,' says Matthew. 'They're really tough, extreme survival experts.'

'The Dry Garden is full of "camel" plants that have adapted to survive in hot, dry conditions such as you get in the Mediterranean basin. They're really tough, extreme survival experts.'

In all, 5500 plants drawn from 850 species and cultivars now thrive in the Dry Garden. In mid-June, the collection is at its best, a living mass of colour and texture, sculpted in flowering spires, feathery grasses and silver-leaved shrubs. As you wander its gravel paths, past clustered purple jewels of *Verbena rigida*, the yellow pompon heads of the Armenian basket flower (*Centaurea macrocephala*) and the red-bristled flowers of pineapple guavas (*Acca sellowiana*), you do feel you have been transported to a dry Mediterranean hillside. 'Since May 2001 it has never been watered, never been fed with fertilizer and never had any pesticides on it of any description. It's probably the lowest-input ornamental garden in the whole of the RHS,' says Matthew.

The RHS is presently assessing its water use across its four gardens. Staff at the RHS garden at Wisley, in Surrey, are allowed to take 50,000 cubic metres (1.8 million cubic feet) of water from the adjacent River Wey, but during times of drought have voluntarily reduced the garden's water use by 40 per cent. The gigantic lake, dug out beside the new Bicentenary Glasshouse, will now act as a back-up supply. Further east, at Hyde Hall, Curator Ian Le Gros has installed water meters so he can monitor exactly how much water is used from the reservoir and how much from the mains. Five years ago, the garden was obtaining two-thirds of its water from the mains and a third from

the reservoir, but now, thanks to improved drainage, it's the other way round. 'We can monitor how much rain we've had and measure the soil moisture,' he says. 'That way we can pick the best time to irrigate and water a set amount. We try to water correctly, by giving a good soaking and watering as much as we can in the mornings and evenings.'

Rosemoor and Harlow Carr are blessed with higher levels of rainfall than the other gardens but are both taking action to conserve what resources they have. Large areas of meadow have been left to grow in both gardens; these do not require watering. At Harlow Carr, which has no irrigation system in place, Matthew Wilson's team have planted 'naturalistic perennials' in borders. These are either species that grow wild somewhere in the world, or fertile hybrids that are similar to their parents and don't require much looking after. 'With traditional herbaceous perennial borders, everything's staked up and watered,' says Matthew. 'Because the plants are grown for their aesthetic value rather than their ability to grow together naturally, you'll have a canna that needs loads of water next to an artemisia that doesn't like water at all. Naturalistic perennials don't need staking, tying-in or deadheading – you just let the cycle go. We've not watered the borders at Harlow Carr for two years.'

ABOVE *The RHS is taking steps to conserve water at each of its gardens*

OVERLEAF *The 'naturalistic perennials' in Harlow Carr's borders provide a spectacular display, without requiring much attention*

Wild about gardens

Aside from preserving water, there is a distinct trend towards increasing biodiversity in gardens, which the RHS is keenly supporting. In 2004 the Society joined forces with The Wildlife Trusts to try to unite the worlds of gardening and nature conservation. Relatively little is known about the environmental value of domestic gardens, so the collaboration aimed to increase our understanding in this field. In 2006 the two organizations conducted a survey, asking people to detail the plants in their gardens, outline their gardening practices, such as mulching and composting, and report sightings of hedgehogs, goldfinches, common frogs, toads and brown bumble-bees. The responses of the 1500 participants suggested that gardeners are beginning to take steps to encourage wildlife into their gardens but that more could be done.

For example, the findings revealed that, while individual garden habitats can be useful wildlife havens, there is greater value to be had from somehow connecting these disparate green oases. Of the gardens visited by all five key species, nearly all had tall trees, but only a third shared other important features such as ponds, log-piles and long grass. The results also showed that gardeners are more likely to take steps to attract birds, hedgehogs and frogs than encourage less popular creepy-crawlies, even though these play a vital role in creating self-sustaining wildlife habitats. Other interesting revelations are: that gardens with seed- or nut-producing plants are three times more likely to attract goldfinches; plots with over 4 sq m (5 sq yards) of long grass are favourable to brown bumble-bees, and London gardens have the lowest average number of sightings of hedgehogs and frogs compared with the rest of the UK. The plan is to repeat the survey over the years and build up a more detailed picture of the contribution UK gardens make to the nation's fauna.

At Wisley, the RHS has set aside a portion of land beside the River Wey as a haven for wildlife. The river flows down from Hampshire, past Guildford, eventually to enter the Thames. As you walk in a northerly direction from the Laboratory building, which houses Wisley's scientific and administrative departments, the formality of colour-coordinated beds and manicured lawns soon gives way to the less groomed landscape of the Pinetum. Here, pines

ABOVE *Water features provide a habitat for insects and amphibians*

OPPOSITE *The plants we choose for our gardens can influence the type of wildlife that comes to visit*

and conifers planted in around 1898 by the garden's original owner, George Fergusson Wilson, contrast with colourful species such as *Acer, Hamamelis* and flowering *Cornus*. The wildlife area stands at the far end of the Pinetum, behind a closed gate. This part of the garden is deliberately kept off-limits to visitors, so the flora and fauna can thrive undisturbed by human activities. 'It was already a natural area that had not really been cultivated,' says Wisley-based RHS principal entomologist Andrew Halstead, as he leads a tour of the area. 'It's a low-lying part of the garden that floods every so often, so it had been pretty much left to its own devices.'

The decision was taken in the mid-1990s to develop 1.2 ha (3 acres) of riverside land as a wildlife sanctuary and manage it with the specific aim of increasing biodiversity. Before it was redeveloped, the area was a woody floodplain, periodically inundated by the river. With the help of the Environment Agency, Wisley's gardeners created an oxbow lake with three islands following a previous course of the river. They placed the spoil they removed across the area to create new habitats. 'At the start there were big mud patches that we allowed to naturally revegetate,' says Andrew. 'That grassy slope there was one of them. There were high levels of nutrients in the river mud, which we are trying to reduce so that eventually the slope will become a wild-flower meadow.'

'It was already a natural area that had not really been cultivated. It's a low-lying part of the garden that floods every so often, so it had been pretty much left to its own devices.'

The area has a rambling, overgrown feel to it. A network of paths, lined with towering hogweed, brambles, nettles, pink campion and the occasional foxglove, is shaded by alder, oak and ash trees. Staff have tried to remove some non-native species such as sycamore seedlings and rhododendrons, although the explosive seed-scattering mechanism of Himalayan balsam (*Impatiens glandulifera*) has enabled this introduced weed firmly to establish itself in the area. 'You get these 6-foot [2-m] tall stems that shade out native flowers but getting rid of it altogether would be a big job,' says Andrew. Of the 350 plant species recorded in the wildlife area, 50 are currently non-native.

Yellow water-lilies (*Nuphar lutea*) and bulrushes (*Schoenoplectus lacustris*) grow along the river, while the pond margins are home to large bittercress

OPPOSITE *More than 50 species of bird have been recorded in Wisley's wildlife area, including herons*

(*Cardamine amara*), brooklime (*Veronica beccabunga*), marsh marigold (*Caltha palustris*) and purple loosestrife (*Lythrum salicaria*). The floor of the drier woodland is painted mauve and white in springtime with bluebells (*Hyacinthoides non-scripta*) and Solomon's seal (*Polygonatum multiflorum*). Other plants typical of woodland habitats include climbing corydalis (*Ceratocapnos claviculata*) and silver hair-grass (*Aira caryophyllea*). Look carefully and you'll even see the rare greater dodder (*Cuscuta europaea*), a parasitic plant that attaches itself to nettles and wild hops, and feeds on their sap using specially adapted suckers. It used to be quite widespread along the Thames Valley, but today it has disappeared from many sites. 'It's surprisingly local,' says Andrew, pointing out the stringy, leafless red-stemmed plant. 'It's here at this exact spot every year, but we never see it 10 yards [9 m or so] away.'

Wisley's staff monitor fungi in the wildlife area twice a year. They have so far recorded over a hundred species, including microscopic rusts and mildews

plus various larger species such as the bracket fungus *Ganoderma adspersum* and toadstools *Armillaria gallica* and *Laccaria laccata*. To date 55 species of bird have been identified at the site, including lesser spotted woodpeckers, treecreepers, mute swans, grey herons and kingfishers. The last named dig nests in the sandy bank of the river and dip into the water to grab fish to feed their new offspring. A pair of swans has twice nested on one of the islands but has yet to produce any cygnets. Other birds that have set up home in the area include kestrels, mandarin ducks and tawny owls. Various mammals, reptiles and amphibians have been recorded, along with ten species of fish. Otters are thought to drop by occasionally. 'We've had sightings of otters, but it's not considered official until we've got

ABOVE *A bee gathers nectar from* Doronicum orientale '*Magnificum*'

solid evidence, such as footprints, droppings or an irrefutable photograph,' says Andrew.

The insect count seems particularly healthy. Andrew is quick to spot a pair of green dock beetles. The female has a noticeably swollen abdomen, while the male is much thinner. Turning over the leaves of the dock plant on which they are sitting, he points out clusters of their yellow eggs. Close by, an alder tree is sporting brown patches on its leaves. Such markings are often caused by insects that live and feed among the epidermal layers of leaves. When Andrew holds a leaf up to the light, a curl of white sawfly larvae is clearly visible in a transparent patch among the veins. Moments later, he deftly catches a cricket sitting in long grass. He explains how you can differentiate a cricket from a grasshopper by looking at the length of its antennae. Cricket antennae are as long as their body, while grasshopper ones are shorter and more sturdy. 'The great thing with insects is that the more you look for them, the more you find,' he says.

By the end of 2006 over 1600 species of invertebrates had been recorded in the wildlife area, over 120 of which are considered to be nationally notable, rare or vulnerable to extinction. Many of these are associated with dead wood or mature trees; when two trees fell down in the wildlife area, staff left them *in situ*, and they have since become a useful habitat for insects such as stag beetles. Two beetles that are classified by the Joint Nature Conservation

ABOVE *Red admiral butterflies alight on* Colletia paradoxa

OVERLEAF *Wisley's Laboratory building attracts bees and nesting house martins, while its flower-rich borders supply nectar to a variety of butterflies*

Committee (JNCC) as vulnerable to extinction, *Lymexylon navale,* a wood-boring beetle, and *Nephus quadrimaculatus,* a tiny ladybird associated with ivy-clad trees, have both been recorded close by. 'Our management of the area is fairly hands off,' says Andrew. 'We are leaving the animals and plants largely to their own devices, although it is necessary to mow paths and periodically cut back some of the shrubby growth to retain open areas.'

Although the wildlife area is specifically managed to lure creatures to it, other parts of the gardens also attract insects, birds, bats and bees. The Laboratory building is a surprisingly popular habitat. House martins build their nests under the eaves, bee swarms colonize some of the chimneys, and several species of bats, including pipistrelles, live in the roof. The nearby canal provides a generous larder of insects for the birds and bats, and a home for the native common frog and larger marsh frog. The flower-rich borders provide nectar for many butterflies including small tortoiseshell, red admiral, peacock and painted lady. They find catmint, sedums, verbenas, sneezeweed (*Helenium*) and coneflower (*Echinacea*) particularly attractive.

Inspiring horticultural excellence

Increasingly, the horticultural practices the RHS employs across all its gardens are aimed at gardening sustainably in a way that encourages biodiversity. Leaving grass long at particular times of year cuts down on water use as well as providing shelter and food for ladybirds, mice and frogs. Whereas once the garden staff removed seed heads and dead foliage, these are now left in place for birds and insects to feast on during the lean winter months. And the deep mulches applied to the borders help to conserve moisture in the soil, suppress weeds and lure worms, beetles and other invertebrates to come and break down the organic matter.

Garden waste is put to good use through composting schemes in all the RHS gardens. At Rosemoor, a large concrete yard is set aside for making compost. There are always several piles in the yard. One contains fresh plant material such as leaves, thin branches and grass; another has large pieces of wood awaiting chipping, and another holds stable litter that is added to the plant material to help the process of decomposition. 'We just let it sit, and it turns itself inexorably into good garden compost,' says Christopher Bailes. It

takes around six to nine months for material to travel the full circle from being pruned from the garden to going back into the soil. Meanwhile, the brown liquor that drains from the decomposing plants collects in a 50,000-litre (11,000-gallon) subterranean concrete tank, before being pumped out and sprayed back on to the warm, rotting heaps.

At Wisley, the RHS has invested in a fermenting machine that it uses to produce an organic liquid feed. The solution contains beneficial micro-organisms that some researchers claim improves root health and plant growth when applied to foliage and roots in a diluted form. Humic compost and sugar are placed in 100 litres (22 gallons) of water and left to brew for 18 hours. Each batch has to be used within 24 hours. Currently, Wisley's gardeners are applying the tea fortnightly to glasshouse crops, but it could in future prove useful in other intensively planted areas such as the rose beds and lawns.

Over the past ten years the Society has slashed its use of fertilizers, pesticides and peat, but it is planning further reductions to improve its green credentials. 'We've been carrying out a very broad and detailed assessment of everything we use in the gardens – ranging from peat through to fertilizer, pesticides and water – with the aim of creating a plan to reduce our use further,' says Jill Cherry. 'We are constantly trying to manage our resources more responsibly, but there's still plenty of work to do. Our gardens are founded on the basis of horticultural excellence. We have constantly to challenge ourselves as to what that horticultural excellence means. I don't think that just means offering the public fabulous gardens. It means providing ones that have been created in the most sustainable way.'

ABOVE *Composting garden trimmings and uncooked vegetable scraps helps reduce the amount of waste sent to landfill sites*

How to make your garden a haven for wildlife

various bees including the red mason bee (*Osmia rufa*), an important pollinator of fruit trees and bushes in gardens.

Butterflies and moths

Make sure you have plants flowering from late winter to autumn in your garden. Stinging nettle (*Urtica dioica*) is the larval-food plant for butterflies such as the red admiral, comma, peacock and small tortoiseshell, while alyssum (*Aurinia saxatilis*) is a popular early nectar plant for butterflies. Autumn-flowering asters and sedums, plus winter-flowering viburnums and mahonias, can help ensure your garden blooms beyond the summer. Planting the meadow wild flower lady's bedstraw (*Galium verum*) will help attract moths.

Bees

Lime trees (*Tilia* species), maples (*Acer* species) and blackberry (*Rubus fruticosus*) all offer a good source of nectar for bees. Providing a safe haven over winter may help conserve our bee populations; of the 25 species of bumble-bee native to Britain and Ireland, three have already become extinct, two are close to extinction and a further nine are declining. Many bumble-bees nest at or below ground level, especially in old mouse holes. You can simulate this environment by sinking an upturned 15-cm (6-in) diameter flowerpot in the ground and covering it with a lid, using a piece of hose-pipe to provide a tunnel up to the soil surface. Bumble-bees can then build a nest in the subterranean chamber you have created. You can also attract solitary bees by providing a nest site made from a bundle of hollow plant stems such as bamboo canes. This will suit

Birds and mammals

Growing plants such as holly, pyracantha, rudbeckia and ornamental grasses will provide berries and seeds to attract birds and small mammals. Mezereon (*Daphne mezereon*) has berries that are a good source of food for greenfinches, while teasel (*Dipsacus fullonum*) is a good winter-food source for all finches. Leave seed heads of annuals and herbaceous perennials over winter to provide both food and shelter for many insects, birds and small mammals. Consider replacing fences with hedges, as this will offer nesting sites as well as additional food sources. Training ivy up walls provides nectar and pollen for autumn insects and berries for birds to eat when there is little else around. Ivy also makes a good nesting place. Install bird nest boxes and bat boxes, and be sure to keep water and food supplies going all year round.

ABOVE *A bumble-bee on a cornflower in the wild-flower beds on Wisley's Fruit Field*

Amphibians

Create a water feature in your garden. Even something small such as a bird-bath or washing-up bowl can provide water for birds for drinking and bathing. A pond will become a spawning ground for slug-eating amphibians and home to insects that attract birds and bats.

Insects

Create a log-pile to provide a habitat for insects and small mammals. Choose scented plants such as mock orange, honeysuckle and night-scented stock to lure insects into your garden at night. Restrict the use of pesticides to situations where their use is really needed. Where available, use natural enemies for biological control or short-lived pesticides based on natural substances. The ladybird is a gardener's friend with its liking for aphids and can be encouraged by planting pollen-rich plants, such as tansy and yarrow, fennel, thyme and dill.

Composting

Put all your old plant material and uncooked vegetable scraps into a compost bin. You can buy one or make one out of old pallets. Cover the contents, and turn it over occasionally with a fork. Eventually, with the help of worms and other creatures, your waste material will turn into compost that you can put back on to the garden.

ABOVE *A log shelter with a fern-covered roof at Harlow Carr provides nooks and crannies for insects to inhabit*

CHAPTER 2
gardening the globe

The present trend towards more sustainable horticultural practices is one of many influences that have shaped our gardens down the centuries. If we were to turn back the clock to the early sixteenth century, we should find gardens that looked very different from today's. At that time, most ornamental plants grown in Britain were native species of Europe and the Mediterranean, such as snake's head fritillary, sea pink and lily of the valley. But as explorers reached lands previously unknown to Europeans, foreign plants began sprouting from the continent's soil. Crocuses, cyclamen, hyacinths and tulips arrived from the Turkish Empire from the 1560s onwards. Within a century, New World explorers had begun supplementing these with new ornamentals such as evening primroses and Michaelmas daisies. Then, from the 1830s, Britain's colonies in India sent back a plethora of exuberantly coloured rhododendrons. Because of this influx of exotics, and the hybrids they yielded as nurserymen got to grips with cultivating their new botanical charges, some 95 per cent of the plants grown in our gardens today are not native to the British Isles.

ABOVE *An early meeting of the Society, seen through the eyes of cartoonist George Cruikshank*

For the past two centuries, the Royal Horticultural Society has been a major influence on the plants grown in British gardens. The Society dates back to 1804 when Sir Joseph Banks, president of the leading scientific academy, the Royal Society, and influential in all fields of science, organized a meeting at Hatchards bookshop in London of six men interested in horticulture. They were John Wedgwood, a banker from the famous pottery family, who later became uncle to Charles Darwin, the royal gardeners William Forsyth of Kensington and St James's palaces and William Townsend Aiton of Kew, nurseryman James Dickson and amateur gardeners Charles Francis Greville and Richard Anthony Salisbury. The group discussed a paper put forward by Wedgwood for the formation of a society devoted to improving horticulture. An extract reads:

> *It is now proposed to institute a Society, for the sole purpose of encouraging Horticulture in its different branches. To form a Repository for all the knowledge, which can be collected on this subject, and to give a stimulus to the exertions of individuals for its farther improvement. It is well known to all persons who have made inquiries on this subject, that there are various facts relative to Gardening, confined to small districts, which would be of general utility. These facts will be collected by the Society, and the knowledge of them dispersed generally over the Country.*

Thus the Horticultural Society of London was born, from which evolved the RHS we know today.

The plant collectors

At the time of the Society's conception, Britain and other European countries were actively exploring the world and bringing back samples of the exotic flora and fauna they encountered. Joseph Banks himself had explored the South Pacific with Captain Cook on board the *Endeavour* between 1768 and 1771 and brought back 1300 new species from 110 new genera. The botanical spoils of such journeys stoked an interest in collecting foreign plants that had emerged in the mid-sixteenth century. 'The influx of exotics began long before Victorian times,' explains Brent Elliott, who, as librarian and archivist at the RHS's Lindley Library in London, has meticulously traced how plants and seeds have ebbed and flowed around the globe for centuries. 'In the 1570s when Flemish botanist Matthias de Lobel first came to England, he found a London apothecary who even at that time had a collection of cacti from the dry tropical regions of the Americas.'

The desire to collect unusual plants had soon spread, with the arrival of tulips from Turkey causing a particular stir. Because it was difficult to predict when a plant was in bulb what colour pattern its petals would exhibit, collectors excitedly anticipated getting a wonderful new variant. 'Records show that some changed hands for the price of a fine carriage and horses,' says Brent. 'No other flower has ever commanded the high prices that tulips fetched during that period.' It was not long before adventurous individuals began forging a career in collecting plants and artefacts from foreign shores. Father-and-son botanists, the John Tradescants, were among the very first, bringing back roses, fritillaries and mulberries from Europe and the tulip tree and a yucca plant from Virginia. Towards the end of the seventeenth century, Henry Compton, bishop of London, was transplanting trees from North America to the grounds of his country retreat of Fulham Palace. Botanist Peter Collinson, who resided at Mill Hill in north London, was also highly influential, bringing in hundreds of American trees to Britain.

'The influx of exotics began long before Victorian times. In the 1570s when Flemish botanist Matthias de Lobel first came to England, he found a London apothecary who even at that time had a collection of cacti from the dry tropical regions of the Americas.'

As collectors experimented to find out which soils, climatic conditions and watering regimes best suited their foreign botanical specimens, gardening began to emerge as a horticultural discipline at which anyone could try their hand. Those needing guidance could seek advice from a burgeoning array of books, such as William Lawson's *A New Orchard and Garden ... With the Country Housewifes Garden for Herbes of Common Use* (1623), John Parkinson's *Paradisi In Sole Paradisus Terrestris* (1629) and John Laurence's *The Clergy-Man's Recreation: Shewing the Pleasure and Profit of the Art of Gardening* (1717). The creation of botanical gardens such as the Chelsea Physic Garden by the Worshipful Society of Apothecaries in 1673 and the

Royal Botanic Gardens at Kew by Princess Augusta in 1759 helped drive interest in gardens and the world's diverse flora. When in 1772, as Kew's unofficial director, Joseph Banks sent one of its collectors and gardeners, Francis Masson, to the Cape of Good Hope in South Africa on the first official mission to collect botanical specimens, he set a trend that was to generate an explosion in the volume of new plants and seeds entering Britain.

Banks and associates initially concentrated on expanding the membership of their embryonic horticultural society and gained a Royal Charter for their efforts in 1809. Then, as Britain's empire expanded and plant-collecting Britons began sending back unusual botanical offerings from the colonies, the Society took charge of a small garden in Kensington. John Reeves, a Canton-based factor for the East India Tea Company, donated an early consignment of plants for the plot from China; Nathaniel Wallich of Calcutta Botanic Gardens later

ABOVE *Early tulip collectors were enthralled by the unpredictable colours and patterns of the petals*

dispatched a selection of Indian plants, and Stamford Raffles sent tropical fruits from the British colony of Singapore he had founded. When, in 1821, the Duke of Devonshire offered a 13-ha (33-acre) site in Chiswick, the Society began sending its own gardeners abroad to seek out and bring home new species. John Potts travelled to China on board the East India Company's ship *General Kyd*, at the invitation of its captain, and sent a consignment of plants to the Society in February 1822. However, he died soon after returning to Britain. George Don then went to Africa and the West Indies and gathered notable plants such as *Nicotiana doniana* (as *N. repanda*, the 'true Havana cigar tobacco'). A third invited collector, John Forbes, died while gathering plants around Africa's Zambezi river, but his name lives on in some of his introductions, such as the orchids *Oncidium forbesii* and *Cattleya forbesii*.

ABOVE *Intrepid plant collectors inspired an interest in gardens and gardening that has continued to this day*

In 1823, the Society instigated its own expedition for the first time. It initially planned to send two men to China, one of whom would return after a year and the other who would stay put for two years. However, having already lost two of its three previous collectors and with the situation in China deemed 'disasterous [*sic*]' in the lead up to the Opium Wars, the Society opted to play safe and send a single representative, John Damper Parks. Aided by Chinese collectors who gathered plants from wild areas off limits to Europeans, Parks sent back yellow forms of the Banksian rose, 16 new chrysanthemum cultivars, *Camellia reticulata* and the first aspidistra (*Aspidistra lurida*) to arrive on English shores. The second collector the Society had planned to send to China was David Douglas, a Scotsman recommended by Glasgow University's professor of botany, William Jackson Hooker. Instead, they instructed him to go to New York to collect fruits and plants from American nurseries. 'David Douglas is the most famous of the RHS's collectors because of the huge range of conifers he introduced, including the Douglas fir that now commemorates him,' says Brent.

Seeds of success

Douglas reached New York in August 1823 and set about exploring the local vegetable markets and flower gardens before heading for the wilds of Buffalo and Amherstburg on Lake Erie. Here he gathered seed from veronicas, eupatoriums, helianthemums, liatris, solidagos and asters. On encountering a tall oak, he used his gun to shoot down branches and collect specimens of the leaves and acorns. Despite being robbed of his money and possessions while climbing a tree to collect seed, and almost sinking with his boat in a storm on the return journey to Buffalo, Douglas travelled onwards towards Philadelphia via Niagara Falls. From there he made his way back to New York, stopping beside the Hudson river to collect insect-devouring sarracenias, or pitcher plants, from a swamp. He reached England in January 1824. When he delivered his collection, including a wide range of ornamentals plus new varieties of apple, pear, plum, peach and grape, the Society hailed his trip as a 'success beyond our expectations'. Within six months they had sent him off again, this time on the Hudson's Bay Company ship *William and Ann* for an eight-and-a-half-month voyage to the mouth of the Columbia river.

The ship stopped at Madeira, Rio de Janeiro, the Juan Fernández islands and the Galapagos islands, allowing Douglas to gather plant material along the way. It eventually arrived at the Columbia river in April 1825. Douglas was to base himself for the next two years at the Hudson's Bay Company headquarters, Fort Vancouver, 145 km (90 miles) up river from the coast. During his first summer there he made short forays into the surrounding countryside to familiarize himself with the local flora and fauna. It was on one such trip that he discovered the conifer that came to bear his name, which, he noted, 'exceeds all trees in magnitude. I measured one lying on the shore of the river 39 feet [12 m] in circumference and 159 feet [48 m] long; the top was wanting … so I judge that it would be in all about 190 feet [60 m] high … they grow very straight; the wood is softer than most … and easily split.' He also encountered the Oregon grape (*Mahonia aquifolium*) and the flowering currant (*Ribes sanguineum*), now both popular garden shrubs favoured for their vibrant spring blossom. As his plant collection expanded, he moved from a tent to a deerskin lodge and finally a bark hut so he could accommodate it.

The conifer 'exceeds all trees in magnitude. I measured one lying on the shore of the river 39 feet in circumference and 159 feet long; the top was wanting … so I judge that it would be in all about 190 feet high.'

Several of the RHS's plant collectors strayed little further than the nurseries and gardens of their host cities in their plant-gathering missions, but Scotsman David Douglas was made of sterner stuff. In June 1825, he embarked on a strenuous month-and-a-half-long journey up the Columbia river, which proved to be an exhausting battle against the wind, weather and currents. Writing in his diary about the conditions he endured in his chosen vocation, Douglas noted:

The luxury of a night's sleep on a bed of pine branches can only be appreciated by those who have experienced a route over a barren plain, scorched by the sun, or fatigued by groping their way through a thick forest, crossing gullies, dead wood, lakes, stones, &c. Indeed so much worn out was I three times by fatigue and hunger that twice I crawled, for I could hardly walk, to a small abandoned hut. I had in my knapsack one biscuit.

During his three-year stay, Douglas covered an extraordinary 11,317 km (7032 miles) of ground.

ABOVE *Plant collector David Douglas introduced the mighty Douglas
fir to Britain from North America in the early nineteenth century*

After two years back in Britain, Douglas returned for what was to be his last visit to North America. He sent home three chest loads of seeds, gathered around the Columbia cascades from trees such as the giant fir (*Abies grandis*), and the silver red fir (*A. amabilis*), before sailing south for California. Here he encountered 360 species and 20 genera previously unknown to the West, including the noble fir (*A. procera*) before returning north in the autumn. After overwintering at his old haunt of Fort Vancouver, Douglas embarked on another ambitious journey but met with disaster when his canoe overturned, and he was plunged into a turbulent whirlpool. Having lost his plant collection and journal in the accident, and by now having also lost the sight in one eye, Douglas sailed for the Sandwich Islands (now Hawaii). Here he climbed Mauna Kea and Mauna Loa but came to a grisly end when he fell into a cattle pit and was gored to death by a bullock. His legacy is the 200-plus species he introduced to Britain, including the so-called 'Californian annuals' such as *Clarkia elegans* and *Eschscholzia californica,* plus the conifer that gave rise to our forestry industry (Sitka spruce – *Picea sitchensis*). Britain's only native conifers are the yew, Scots pine and common juniper; many of the other stately evergreens that now dominate our landscapes are there thanks to Douglas's tireless wanderings in a distant and inhospitable land.

The same year that Douglas had returned to England after his first expedition, an opportunity arose for an RHS-sponsored collector to go to the Sandwich Islands. Kamehameha II, the king of the Sandwich Islands, and his

ABOVE *Douglas also introduced 'Californian annuals' such as* Eschscholzia californica, *seen here at Hyde Hall*

queen, Kamamalu, died in England after contracting measles while on a state visit to George IV. Captain George Byron was dispatched to carry the bodies back to Honolulu for burial, accompanied by gardener James MacRae, who was to bring gifts of fruit trees and other plants to the islands. After stops in Brazil and Chile, their ship the *Blonde* arrived in the Sandwich Islands, where the royal funerals were conducted. It then returned via the Galapagos Islands, Peru and Chile, providing MacRae with ample plant-gathering opportunities. Like his predecessors, MacRae introduced mainly tropical species, including hippeastrums, alstroemerias, *Cleome rosea* and *Oxalis plumieri*. On his return to England he was made a corresponding member of the Society and headed to Ceylon, now Sri Lanka, to take up the post of superintendent at Peradeniya Botanic Garden in 1826. He died in 1830, four years ahead of Douglas.

Hardy plants for the ornamental garden

Before Douglas's journeys to North America, it had been the norm for plant collectors to concentrate on gathering tropical species that would be nurtured in the greenhouse on arrival on Britain's chilly shores. But the Scotsman's introduction of so many species that could tolerate the British conditions helped change the emphasis for future collectors. From now on, hardy plants for the ornamental garden became the primary objects of botanists' desire. In 1836, the Society instructed German botanist Carl Theodore Hartweg to travel to Mexico and gather plants at altitudes likely to yield hardy or at least half-hardy varieties. The only exception to this rule was for orchids, which were becoming increasingly popular. By the time he arrived back in England, after visiting Mexico, Guatemala, Ecuador, Peru, Colombia and the Caribbean, he had sent back 65 new species of orchid and sufficient conifer seeds for the Society to distribute 4300 packets to fellows and botanic gardens.

Hartweg returned to Mexico and California in 1845 with instructions to track down *Zauschneria*, which he duly did. We also have him to thank for *Lupinus affinis* and *L. hartwegii*, various penstemons, Mexican cacti and ceanothus, plus conifers such as *Cupressus macrocarpa*, *Sequoia sempervirens* and several pines. His success may be due in part to his competitive nature, as illustrated by this quote from Theodor Cordua, published in an article in *Leaflets of Western Botany*:

I have often heard him say that Mr George Ure Skinner [an orchid collector] and himself discovered the large plant of Laelia superbiens *both at the same time when in Mexico, and that they were both determined to have it, but could not get it then, for it was up a very high tree. Hartweg outwitted Mr Skinner by going early in the morning, taking with him a native and an axe, and chopping the tree down, at the same time conveying away the large Laelia. I recollect helping to unpack it at Chiswick on its arrival, and it just filled one large wooden case, and arrived in excellent health.*

During the early nineteenth century, the success or failure of plant-collecting trips was as much to do with the arrangements for transporting plants and seeds home as with the skills and tenacity of the collector. Sea journeys were often long and arduous, with plants being either at risk of too little sunlight if stored below decks or at the mercy of sea spray if left open to the elements. However, from 1830 onwards, transporting plants became

ABOVE *Nathaniel Bagshaw Ward's glazed Wardian case revolutionized the transportation of plants*

much easier, thanks to the invention of the Wardian case by Nathaniel Bagshaw Ward. This was a glazed box, in which plants, soil and water formed a self-sustaining environment, protected from the outside elements. From Hartweg on, all the RHS's collectors were equipped with Wardian cases in which to place the spoils of their adventures. Such was the influence of the Society at this time that garden journalist John Claudius Loudon said that the majority of plants that had been introduced to British gardens in the last quarter of a century had come through the RHS. 'We had such a large number of collectors all operating in the same decade and a half that we had a disproportionate share of the importation market,' says Brent Elliott. 'We sent collectors to every continent except Australia.'

Eastern ambitions and the modern day

Until the early nineteenth century, China's sheer size and strength had kept the colonizing nations of Portugal, Britain, Spain and Holland at bay. However, by 1840, Britain was emerging as the most powerful nation in the world and felt it was time it had a share of the Orient's rich pickings. At the time, British merchants were making their fortunes by smuggling opium from British India into China. When the Chinese attempted to enforce her laws against the trade, conflict broke out. The superior strength of the British military won them two separate wars in the mid-1800s. Following the first, the Treaty of Nanking in 1842 ceded Hong Kong to Britain as well as opening up the ports of Shanghai, Ningpo (Ningbo), Foochow (Fuzhou) and Amoy (Xiamen) to Western trade. After the second, the Chinese legalized the import of opium and granted a number of privileges to British and other Western subjects within China. One British citizen who took advantage of this was Thomas Hanbury. He accrued wealth as a silk and tea merchant in China, which, much later, enabled him to buy the Wisley estate and donate it to the RHS in 1903.

Meanwhile, the changed circumstances in China meant British plant collectors could now investigate the botanical treasures of areas previously off limits to them. Recognizing this opportunity, the Society dispatched Scottish botanist Robert Fortune, the first student to gain distinction in the Society's examinations, to Hong Kong: his instructions were to gather hardy plants such as 'the Peaches of Pekin' [*sic*], 'plants that yield tea', 'double yellow roses',

OVERLEAF *The Rock Garden was developed shortly after merchant Thomas Hanbury donated Wisley to the RHS in 1903*

'varieties of Nelumbium' and 'peonies with blue flowers'. During Fortune's three years in China he was robbed several times, attacked by pirates and narrowly missed falling into a pit designed to trap wild boar. However, he became enchanted by the dazzling azaleas, clematis and honeysuckles of the Chusan Islands, eventually drawing the conclusion that China is 'the central flowery land'. From this first visit he sent back the yellow-flowering winter jasmine (*Jasminum nudiflorum*), *Forsythia viridissima*, *Mahonia japonica*, *Viburnum plicatum*, the lace-bark pine (*Pinus bungeana*), bleeding heart (*Dicentra spectabilis*) and a host of azaleas, camellias, tree peonies and bamboos. Other introductions that now decorate our gardens thanks to him include the mourning cypress (*Cupressus funebris*) and *Rhododendron fortunei,* in which the adventurous plant collector's name lives on.

After Fortune, the RHS sent two more individual plant collectors abroad: Matteo Botteri, who sent back *Chamaecyparis* specimens from Mexico, and John Weir, who collected plants 'of minor interest', according to the Society's proceedings, from Brazil. Following these expeditions, two nursery-organized trips to the Chinese interior prompted a further flurry of exploration to both the

Orient and the Himalayas. During the early years of the twentieth century, collectors such as George Forrest, Ernest Henry Wilson and Frank Kingdon-Ward made their names gathering new varieties of rhododendrons and camellias.

However, the days of individually funded expeditions were over; instead nurseries and organizations such as the Society now contributed to syndicates in exchange for a proportion of the plants and seeds gathered.

'In terms of things being grown for the garden, the nineteenth century saw the discovery of most things that were decently showy.'

'In terms of things being grown for the garden, the nineteenth century saw the discovery of most things that were decently showy,' says Brent Elliott. 'Western China and the Himalayas became the really big focus for garden plant introductions in the early twentieth century, because until this time those regions were off limits to Europeans. The things that have come from elsewhere since have been of a smaller and less showy nature simply because everything that was obviously garden-worthy got grabbed first.'

ABOVE *Trade ships in harbour in the Orient during the nineteenth century, a key time for the great plant collectors*

Some new additions have none the less made it into British gardens in recent years, including the dawn redwood (*Metasequoia glyptostroboides*), which was discovered in 1941 in a tiny village in Szechuan, China, and not identified as a living species until some five years later, and the Catacol whitebeam (*Sorbus pseudomeincichii*), found by researchers on the Scottish Isle of Arran in June 2007. Another recent find is the Wollemi pine (*Wollemia nobilis*). It was discovered in 1994 when New South Wales National Parks and Wildlife Officer David Noble came across a cluster of unusual trees in a rainforest gorge within the Wollemi National Park in the Blue Mountains of Australia. Subsequent morphological studies, wood analysis and DNA testing indicated the tree was an entirely new genus, falling between two previously known living genera, *Agathis* and *Araucaria*. Thought to be long extinct, the Wollemi pine is estimated to be between 90 million and 200 million years old. Thanks to modern propagation techniques, the tree has already made the leap from unknown species to commercially available garden plant and is now on sale in RHS Wisley's plant centre. Royalties from the sale of specimens here and at other outlets are going to support conservation of the Wollemi pine and other rare plant species.

Modern-day plant collecting is primarily carried out by botanical gardens, although a few dedicated individuals still travel afar to gather botanical specimens. These include the author, broadcaster and RHS Floral 'B' Committee member Roy Lancaster, who took part in expeditions to Nepal and Yunnan, China, specifically to collect seeds of plants suitable for Western gardens. Among the expedition finds were a bizarre snowball plant and a rare golden edelweiss. The Society continues to provide bursaries for expeditions that aim to increase our knowledge of endangered and endemic plants worldwide and their cultivation and conservation. For example, in 2004, it supported a five-person expedition to China to retrace the route undertaken by Irish plant hunter Dr Augustine Henry. Organized in collaboration with the Wuhan Botanic Gardens and the Chinese Academy, the expedition visited the species-rich Shennongjia mountain range and the area around Yichang, where Henry had lived and collected for seven years. Other recent RHS-supported projects include a study tour of the Valdivian rainforest areas of Chile, to increase knowledge for UK cultivation, and an expedition to Belize to study Orchidaceae, Arecaceae, Bromeliaceae and Cactaceae for research and collecting purposes.

RIGHT *Today, plant collectors are restricted to gathering seeds*

Although most genera of plants are believed now to have been discovered, future expeditions to little-known areas such as Papua New Guinea and the eastern side of the Andes mountains in South America may yet yield botanical surprises. Plant collecting today, though, is a completely different ball game from that of its Victorian heyday. Growing concerns about the extinction of species during the early twentieth century prompted the founding of the International Union for the Conservation of Nature (IUCN) in 1948. The IUCN published several 'red lists' highlighting endangered plants and animals and lobbied for an international agreement of the traffic in wildlife. As a result, the Convention on the International Trade in Endangered Species of Wild Fauna and Flora (CITES) came into force in 1975 imposing restrictions on the sale of red-list species. Nowadays, the primary rule of plant collecting is that plants must be left *in situ*; only their seeds can be taken away. Keen to promote preservation of wild flora, the RHS is a member of Botanic Gardens Conservation International (BGCI), a worldwide network promoting plant conservation, environmental education and sustainable development.

Creating new cultivars

The multicultural mix of plants that we now grow in our gardens is not only thanks to plant collectors, however. As the flow of new genera and species entering Britain increased in the early nineteenth century, so nurseries started trying to create new varieties through hybridization. This is the process by which cross-breeding two distinct species yields a new variety. For example, *Spartina* x *townsendii* is the result of cross-breeding *Spartina maritima* (British cord grass) and the North American species *Spartina alterniflora*. Hybrids can be fertile or sterile depending on differences in the genomes of the two parents. 'Hybridization has been going on for thousands of years only we don't have records of it, and most of it was accidental,' explains Brent Elliott. 'Virtually all the major staple crops that mankind has are of hybrid origin but were given species names by European botanists who knew no better. But, as my predecessor William Thomas Stearn used to point out, if the annual sowing of wheat stopped for six years we would lose the cultivated wheat that we know, because in six breeding generations it reverts to the wild type, and we don't know the stages by which modern wheat was bred.'

It was not until the 1730s that the first deliberate man-made hybrid was created. This was a dianthus, or pink, bred by London nurseryman Thomas Fairchild, which became known as Fairchild's mule on account of it being sterile. He and a few others experimented with breeding other plants, but it was not until the last decade of the century that a deliberate programme of hybridization aimed at generating new garden plants got under way. This was instigated by Tooting-based nurseryman William Rollison who began breeding Cape heaths, *Erica* species from South Africa. By 1826 he had bred 285 varieties.

'Part of the real reason that people did not hybridize plants systematically until this time is that they were not aware that plants had sexes,' says Brent. 'The only plants that the ancient world recognized as having distinct sexes were palms. In the seventeenth and early eighteenth century there were a number of authors who speculated that plants reproduced sexually, but there was a certain amount of shock value attached to this discovery. When the Swedish botanist Carl Linnaeus based his systematic classification on the number of sexual organs a plant had, some people responded by saying he was decadent and corruptor of morals for emphasizing the sexuality of plants.'

Around the turn of the century, the RHS's second president, Thomas Andrew Knight, put forward the idea that varieties of fruit have natural life cycles. This was prompted by reports that some of the older established English apples, such as 'Ribston Pippin', were deteriorating in quality. Although the theory was wrong, it helped stimulate new experiments in hybridization. A flurry of new soft fruits became available, and the experiments prompted nurserymen to try creating new hybrids of garden plants. One enthusiastic amateur was The Revd William Herbert, rector of Spofforth in Yorkshire and later dean of Manchester, who produced a number of 'azaleodendrons'. The Society acted as a conduit for botanists and nurserymen to share their experiences. As well as frequently publishing the results of experiments in its publications *Transactions of the Horticultural Society of London* and the *RHS Journal,* it was involved in organizing two conferences on hybridization, one held over two days at the garden at Chiswick and Westminster Town Hall, London, in 1899, the other in New York in 1903.

As more nurserymen began to understand the science behind hybridization and selective breeding, they started growing particular types of plant to meet the demands of gardeners. In the 1820s and 1830s there was a growing

OPPOSITE *Many staple crops, including wheat, were produced through hybridization*

enthusiasm for bright colours presented in large masses, but most of the plants available for growing in flower-beds at the time had relatively small flowers in comparison to the size of the plant. 'Early pelargoniums tended to be rather woody-stemmed plants with relatively small flowers, so most of the bed would have been green or brown,' says Brent. 'But once the demand was there the nurserymen began selectively breeding to increase the size of the flower in relation to the rest of the plant. During the course of the 1840s what we recognize now as bedding varieties of pelargoniums, petunias, verbenas and calceolarias appeared on the market, and for the first time you really could get a bed that was a solid mass of one colour.'

ABOVE *Beds of colourful plants became fashionable during the first half of the nineteenth century, as seen in this view of the Parterre at Harewood House*

Disappearing plants

Changes in fashions, technologies and the nation's circumstances have also caused some plants introduced by early plant hunters or cultivated by nurserymen to disappear from our gardens. One influence on the waxing and waning of sub-tropical plants has been the changing use of glasshouses. During the early nineteenth century conservatories tended to be heated by external boilers that emitted hot air through vents into the greenhouse or by internal braziers. This generated an atmosphere that was hot and dry. When methods changed to steam and then hot-water heating, the resulting atmosphere tended to be hot and moist. As a result, lots of the Australian and South African plants that arrived in British gardens in the late eighteenth and mid-nineteenth century simply disappeared from cultivation.

The introduction of coal rationing during the First World War also depleted stocks of conservatory plants. An emblematic story is that of Chatsworth House, whose owner the Duke of Devonshire commissioned one of the greatest glasshouses in the world in the 1830s. Because his descendant who was Duke at the time of the war was not able to argue for an extra coal ration, his collection of sub-tropical plants died during winter 1917, and he decided in 1920 that it would be cheaper to destroy the greenhouse than restock it. Trying to prevent the loss of valuable plant collections during the Second World War, the RHS set up the Non-edible Plants (Fuel) Committee, which sent a team of prominent gardeners around the country to look at all applications for non-reductions or increases in coal rations. 'Their role was to advise on which of the plant collections they visited were so vital they deserved the extra coal,' says Brent.

'Their role was to advise on which of the collections of plants they visited were so important they deserved the extra coal.'

After the Second World War, changing patterns of plant marketing and increased costs of production meant that many nurseries cut back on the breadth of stock they offered. Meanwhile, the price of labour made private gardens increasingly difficult to maintain. Such was the concern about the resulting loss of variety within horticulture by the late 1970s that the RHS organized a conference on 'The practical role of gardens in the conservation

OVERLEAF *National collections of plants such as crocus and snowdrops are helping preserve species and cultivars that might otherwise be lost*

of rare and threatened plants'. The meeting gave rise to the National Council for the Conservation of Plants and Gardens (NCCPG) and laid down plans for the formation of National Plant Collections as a means of preserving plant material. The intention was that such collections would each be 'as complete a representation of a genus or section of a genus as possible'.

'The aim was to conserve cultivated plants because, as time goes on, plants come in and out of fashion and we lose them,' explains Chloe Hughes, administration coordinator for the NCCPG. 'People decide they don't like a particular plant in the garden any more, so that variety gets taken off the shelves of the big garden centres and becomes lost. Chrysanthemum is one genus where many cultivars have been lost because of fashion.'

Today, there are some 660 National Plant Collections representing 358 genera. The parties that hold them range from keen enthusiasts who grow them in private gardens to the National Trust, botanic gardens and local councils. The RHS gardens at Wisley, Rosemoor, Hyde Hall and Harlow Carr

hold 12 National Plant Collections among them. Wisley hosts collections of *Crocus*, *Epimedium*, *Galanthus*, heathers and rhubarb; Rosemoor maintains collections of *Cornus* and *Ilex*; Hyde Hall has the collection of *Viburnum*; Harlow Carr maintains collections of rhubarb, *Polypodium* and *Dryopteris* and *Fuchsia* section *Quelusia*. Every year, for the past two decades, the RHS has published all the plants available commercially in its publication *The RHS Plant Finder*. When staff at the NCCGP recently perused it for crocus species they discovered that 26 once listed are no longer available. Of them, only six were not included in a National Collection, which means 20 species that are no longer commercially available have been saved for posterity. As more National Collections are created, the hope is to stem, and if possible reverse by re-introductions, the loss of our gardening heritage. With continued hard work and good fortune, the tireless dedication of the plant collectors and nurserymen responsible for the eclectic mix of plants found in British gardens today will not have been in vain.

What's in a name?

You might know the tree in your garden as a weeping willow or as *Salix babylonica,* but do you know how it came to be so named? The tree derives its name from Psalm 137, 'By the rivers of Babylon', which laments the exile of the Israelites into unfriendly Babylonia. According to the verse, they weep beneath the willow trees on the river banks of Babylonia, hence the name. In fact, the trees were poplars, not willows; the name ultimately derives from an incorrect translation of the psalm from the Hebrew. Today, most trees we call weeping willows in the UK are a hybrid of the Chinese cultivar *Salix babylonica* 'Pendula', the true weeping willow, and the European white willow (*Salix alba*). It is an example of how inexact a science naming plants can be, even today.

Until the nineteenth century there were no rules for naming plants, but once people began publishing botanical books it became obvious a naming scheme was required. Initially, descriptive monikers were used, which worked well for plants that were relatively distinct but was less useful for categories such as grasses or primulas, where different species have very similar characteristics. 'Sometimes you had different names with the same words in them just because botanists disagreed over whether it was more important to say "prickly-leaved" or "red-flowered" first,' explains Brent Elliott. 'This made finding things in an index quite difficult. As early as 1621 the first dictionary of synonyms of plant names was published.'

In 1753, the Swedish botanist Carl Linnaeus put forward the idea that plant names didn't need to be descriptive; if you had a name for the genus and a name for the species, you could simply look up the description. This meant that names could be more arbitrary, so a plant could be named after a location or the name of the person who introduced it to the West. Linnaeus published *Species Plantarum* ('The species of plants') using his new binomial versions of names of all known plants alongside a description. He used Latin, which was the language of international communication at that time. As new plants were found, Linnaeus and his successors revised his publication, but when it reached multiple volumes it was becoming unwieldy.

CAROLI LINNÆI
S:æ R:giæ M:tis Sveciæ Archiatri; Medic. & Botan.
Profess. Upsal; Equitis aur. de Stella Polari;
nec non Acad. Imper. Monspel. Berol. Tolos.
Upsal. Stockh. Soc. & Paris. Coresf.

SPECIES PLANTARUM,

EXHIBENTES
PLANTAS RITE COGNITAS,
AD
GENERA RELATAS,
CUM
Differentiis Specificis,
Nominibus Trivialibus,
Synonymis Selectis,
Locis Natalibus,
Secundum
SYSTEMA SEXUALE
DIGESTAS.
TOMUS I.

Cum Privilegio S. R. M:tis Sueciæ & S. R. M:tis Poloniæ ac Electoris Saxon.

HOLMIÆ,
Impensis LAURENTII SALVII.
1753.

ABOVE *Linnaeus's* Species Plantarum *listed all plant species known in 1753*

In 1866 the RHS helped organize the first International Botanical Congress, held in London. At the conference it was proposed that there should be a formal set of rules governing the naming of plants. The First International Code of Botanical Nomenclature was published the following year. This stated that every plant should have a generic name and specific epithet, and that these should be in Latin. It was later decided that the date of Linnaeus's *Species Plantarum*, 1753, should be the start date for the new rules. No previous names have any validity today.

The conference also decided that the first published description should determine the name of a plant. However, often the first publication did not have a description attached, so from 1866 it was taken that the first publication of the name together with its description should be the official name. Names coined before 1866 were allowed to stand even if they did not have a proper description accompanying them first time round. Given the veritable flood of plants that had entered Britain at the hands of Victorian plant collectors in the first

half of the nineteenth century, the wholesale renaming of plants would have been too complicated to contemplate.

As well as laying down guidelines for the names of naturally occurring plant species, the 1866 congress also decreed there should be a formally recognized way to identify plants raised through cultivation. It was suggested that these names should not be in Latin but in some other language. They were called 'fancy names'. That favourite British staple, *Solanum tuberosum* 'King Edward', is an example. 'Today, older Latinate names can still stand, but cultivar names are now vernacular terms given in English, French, German, Japanese or some other language,' says Brent.

Along with the style and language applied to naming plants, there is also a formally recognized system for writing names. For species, the genus and species are italicized, and the generic name is capitalized. Cultivar names are given in Roman type and in single quotation marks and are capitalized according to the normal rules for the language. So the species we know by the common name of silver

ABOVE *'A Tribute to Linnaeus' garden at the 2007 Chelsea Flower Show commemorated the tercentenary of the renowned Swedish botanist*

ABOVE *Carl Linnaeus, father of modern taxonomy, surveys the garden created in his honour at Chelsea Flower Show, 2007*

birch is formally identified in Latin as *Betula pendula*, while a weeping cultivar of the silver birch is *Betula pendula* 'Tristis'. It is also generally acceptable to write the generic and cultivar name, as in *Betula* 'Tristis'.

The naming system has generally worked well, but occasional discrepancies have arisen. Way back when Linnaeus was putting together his universal list of plant species, he assigned the name *Chrysanthemum* to a couple of European perennials with small, yellow flowers. When plant collectors introduced morphologically similar plants with much larger flowers from China and Japan these, too, were placed under the *Chrysanthemum* umbrella. However, in the 1960s, botanists scrutinized the genus for the first time and identified 11 discrete genera.

In addition to *Chrysanthemum*, there were now unfamiliar genera such as *Argyranthemum*, *Rhodanthemum* and *Leucanthemum*. Meanwhile, the

chrysanthemum now belonged to a different genus and had to have a different name. So European chrysanthemums are now known as *Glebionis*.

Another change of name, which captures a piece of wartime history, is recorded in letters in one of the box files that line the walls of the plant-trials administration department in Wisley's Laboratory building. The first, dated 13 December 1945, was sent from the RHS to Messrs B. Ruys Ltd in Dedemsvaart, Holland, regarding a phlox the nursery had originally named as Frau Alfred von Mauthner. It notes: 'Our attention has been drawn to the fact that Messrs Bees, of 173 Mill Street, Liverpool 8, have renamed the above-mentioned Phlox and now call it 'Spitfire'.' Usually such a name change would not have been allowed, but the original was not strictly valid because it broke nomenclatural code stating that varietal names should be no more than three words. Therefore, the RHS declared, it was happy to allow the change.

The reply, dated 27 December 1945, agrees:

In reply to your letter of December 13th we beg to inform you that we named Phlox paniculata *Frau Alfred von Mauthner [sic] after a Hungarian Lady who was a great amateur of flowers. However as this Lady was of Jewish origin, it may be that she has disappeared during the last years. At present there are no connections whatever between Holland and Hungary. We agree with you that the name 'Frau Alfred von Mauthner' is exactly speaking not valid and therefore we have no objection against another name which is more intelligible and easier to pronounce for the English speaking peoples. Also in our opinion 'Spitfire' is a very good name and we agree with the renaming of this* Phlox *in [sic]* Spitfire.

big, flashy, oriental plants that people commonly recognized as chrysanthemums became known as *Dendranthema*. But that was not the end of the matter. In the 1990s an RHS committee member lobbied a motion that *Chrysanthemum* be retained as the generic name for the oriental cultivars because of their popularity as garden flowers and the financial losses the confusion of name change might engender. His motion was upheld, which meant Linnaeus's original yellow-flowered

RHS GARDEN TOUR **WISLEY**
with Curator Jim Gardiner

“The most diverse plant collection in the world”

Situated some 30 km (20 miles) southwest of London, Wisley is the Royal Horticultural Society's longest-standing garden, having been donated to the Society by Quaker philanthropist and lover of plants Sir Thomas Hanbury in 1903. Today, it is a garden of gardens, its compartments fashioned gradually through the years by a succession of curators. For the past 20 years, that role has been held by Jim Gardiner, who arrived just after the great storm of 1987. Turning the loss of numerous trees as a result of the storm into an opportunity, he redeveloped damaged areas and began formulating plans for a new great glasshouse that would attract more visitors to Wisley.

'Wisley has the most diverse plant collection in the world,' Jim says. 'It's a garden that meets everyone's needs. You might come here because you just want to relax among fantastic plants or because you're a horticultural student learning to identify species or because you want to get ideas for what to put in your herbaceous border. There's something for everyone.'

If you walk straight ahead when you pass through Wisley's turnstiles, you soon reach red-tiled Weather Hill Cottage, which houses Jim's office. If you were to go inside, you would find shelves crammed with books, such as *Trees and their Bark* and *Subtropical Gardens*, a large board denoting the divisions Jim manages, including Fruit, Glass and Floral, and a mud-encrusted pair of wellingtons. Immediately across the path from the cottage's wrought-iron gates lies the Country Garden. Here, symmetrical paths divide beds containing euphorbias and flowering crab apples, while wisteria creeps its way over a metal arch.

'Each of the beds can be used as a model for smaller gardens or you can emulate the Country Garden as a whole,' says Jim. Running along the garden's eastern side is 'one of the longest mixed borders in the world'. The delightful mêlée of herbaceous, woody and climbing plants is designed to flower first in pastel shades, then hot fiery colours, then pastel again as the long weeks of summer progress.

Passing among the mixed borders, you begin the gentle ascent of Battleston Hill, at the apex of which sits Henry Moore's *The Arch*. Straight ahead is the Portsmouth Trials Field, where the Society puts the latest cultivars through their paces in search of perfectly performing garden plants. Those that make the grade receive the Award of Garden Merit (AGM). If you visit in summer, you'll witness a kaleidoscope of colour as sweet peas, delphiniums, dianthus and irises bloom in close succession. East of the Trials Field the formality of trim, rectangular beds gives way to meandering paths that dissect a hillside of rhododendrons, azaleas, eucalyptus and Jim's speciality, magnolias.

'I've had a great interest in magnolias since I first saw them in the Valley Gardens at Windsor [Great Park] in the late 1960s,' he says. 'This one here is

OPPOSITE *The Bicentenary Glasshouse has created new vistas at Wisley*

Magnolia 'Gold Star',' a hybrid created in the USA by Phil Savage [a well-known plant breeder] from *M. acuminata* 'Miss Honeybee' and *M. stellata* 'Rubra'. Phil sent us some scions for grafting, which I didn't think would have much chance of success. However, they survived, and I became the first person to introduce 'Gold Star' to Europe. We now have four or five growing throughout Wisley, and there are a large number around the world.'

If, rather than climbing Battleston Hill, you continue in a westerly direction from the Country Garden, you'll encounter the Alpine Display and Landscape houses standing side by side. Enter the former at any time of year and you'll see at least one thing in flower, be it elegant *Lilium mackliniae* with its

impetuously up-curled pink petals and jiggling stamen, the azure-flowered dwarf *Delphinium tatsienense* or the luminous orange *Calochortus kennedyi*. 'We grow everything behind the scenes, then, when it comes into flower, we put it out here,' says Jim. 'For every square metre [10 sq feet] of flowers on this bench we need 10 square metres [100 sq feet] behind the scenes.' In the Landscape House, boulders of limestone tufa from Wrexham in North Wales provide beds for plants that need free-draining soil. Embedded in the gravel topping are tiny red rosettes of *Sempervivum* 'Pumaros' and starburst clumps of *Clematis marmoraria*.

Southwest of the glasshouses, extending to Wisley's outer extremities, is the Fruit Field. It covers

some 6.5 ha (16 acres) and hosts 660 cultivars of apples, 100 cultivars of plums and 125 cultivars of pears. Around the borders are espalier-trained soft-fruit trees, such as an outstretched Cristalina 'Sumnue', heavily laden with luscious, sweet cherries. 'We have a living library of fruit growing in our orchards,' says Jim. 'There are examples that date back to Roman times alongside modern commercially available varieties.' Taking a leaf out of the Romans' book, the Society has planted a vineyard of Phönix and Orion grape varieties on a sunny south-facing slope. It plans to produce a batch of wine in collaboration with Plumpton College, a college which specializes in land-based courses, such as horticulture and agriculture, based near Lewes in

East Sussex. Eventually, Jim hopes there will be enough to sell in Wisley's shop.

If you skirt the nearside of the Fruit Field and then turn northeast, you find yourself at the top of the Rock Garden, looking out over a narrow pond to the mature deciduous trees of the Wild Garden beyond. The Rock Garden was one of the first features to be built at Wisley, in 1910. Constructed by specialists James Pulham and Sons, it was a major engineering feat requiring a railway to be built from the nearest road (now the A3) through the Fruit Field. Pulham achieved its natural-looking appearance by replicating the positions of the sandstone blocks before they were quarried. Today, gravel paths wind downhill past delicate auburn maples, burgundy Red Baron grasses (*Imperata cylindrica* 'Rubra') and mauve cushions of *Campanula* planted amid the boulders and ponds. At the bottom lies the Alpine Meadow, which, in spring, is coloured sulphur yellow with *Narcissus* but later turns mauve with autumn-flowering crocus. 'We keep the grass long until August and then cut it and rake it off and use the grass as a mulch around some of the trees,' explains Jim. 'Then we keep it short until the crocus have flowered in September. Keeping the grass long in July and early August helps boost the biodiversity.'

Beside the Alpine Meadow is a small wooden bridge, beneath which mottled black and tangerine carp ripple among white water-lilies. A path leads across it into the Wild Garden, the most historic part of Wisley. This is where, between 1878 and 1902, a previous owner of the land that comprises the garden, the Victorian businessman, scientist, inventor and keen experimental gardener George Fergusson Wilson, made 22,000 separate plantings with the aim of 'growing difficult plants successfully'. Although much altered down the

LEFT *Water-lilies float on the pond beside the Alpine Meadow*

years, the Wild Garden remains true to this ethos. It was originally called Oakwood but lost many of its mature trees in the 1987 storm. Since then, Wisley's staff have planted new oaks and ornamental trees among the existing rhododendrons, bamboo and camellias to restore cover for shade-loving hostas and primulas. The water-table is naturally high here; cream curls of arum lilies and purple-streaked irises both thrive in the boggy soil, and bullfinches splash happily through the shallow puddles at their roots.

The area of Seven Acres that lies beyond the Wild Garden was regarded as useless for cultivation until, in the 1920s, an iron pan (an accumulation of iron oxide) was discovered lying just beneath the surface of the soil. Once it was broken up, plant roots were able to penetrate the soil and suck up water, so staff planted several specimen trees. These now skirt a wide area of lawn and two lakes. A focal point is a six-sided Chinese Pavilion, with sturdy, golden, upright timbers supporting a coal-coloured, upturned roof. 'Two years ago at the Hampton Court Flower Show, China exhibited for the first time,' explains Jim. 'When the show was over, they donated the pavilion to us. Its upright timbers are carved from *Metasequoia*, and it's now standing next to living *Metasequoia* trees.' Over the next few years, Jim plans to plant more trees around the ponds, with springtime varieties at the western end, summer ones at the eastern end and autumn and winter ones scattered around.

From Seven Acres, you can either follow the course of the River Wey into the Pinetum or

complete a circuit of the garden, walking past the Canal and Laboratory to the entrance gate. The Laboratory was built between 1914 and 1916 and houses the Society's scientists, administrative departments and a small lecture theatre. It was built using materials recycled from crumbling manor houses. The Canal now contains one of the largest collections of water-lilies in the world, some 56 hardy cultivars, including the intensely pink *Nymphaea* 'Ellisiana' and the primrose-yellow *N.* 'Texas Dawn'.

'This area was where the original glasshouse was when the Society moved from Chiswick in 1904,' explains Jim. 'When that came to the end of its life the area was redeveloped by landscape architects Sir Geoffrey Jellicoe and Lanning Roper. This year we had to reline the Canal, which involved lifting out all the large containers of water-lilies and replanting them. It took us three weeks.'

Since the Canal was developed in the 1960s, the view of its glassy surface reflecting the half-timbered Laboratory has become the iconic view of Wisley. However, that status may soon be usurped by a new figurehead. During 2006 and early 2007, the Society's new Bicentenary Glasshouse slowly rose from a disused field beyond the Wild Garden on Wisley's western edge. Set beside a new lake, amid a formal garden landscaped by award-winning designer Tom Stuart-Smith, it was opened by HM the Queen in June 2007. Now, its white curvaceous frame and glinting glass panels dominate the skyline as you look west from the Rock Garden. For Jim, the glasshouse is the culmination of more than ten years' planning and will be the lasting legacy of his time as curator.

'The glasshouse was an opportunity to develop the garden and broaden the spread of people visiting,' he says. 'The Society has a great history of growing plants under glass, and our aim is to widen people's awareness of what they can grow. It's been a tremendous privilege to be involved from the start – and great fun too.'

ABOVE *The Chinese Pavilion originally formed part of China's first exhibit at the Hampton Court Palace Flower Show*

OPPOSITE *Wisley's Laboratory was built between 1914 and 1916, and the Canal, in which it is reflected, in the 1960s*

entertaining with plants

Above all the Royal Horticultural Society is known for its flower shows. Every year it puts on 20 or so events, including the major crowd-pullers of Chelsea, Hampton Court and Tatton Park, plus smaller specialist or regional events that include the London Orchid Show, BBC Gardeners' World Live and the Malvern Spring Gardening Show. The events provide an opportunity for floral and garden designers to showcase their latest creations, for nurserymen to display new cultivars and hybrids and for the public to come and peruse the exhibits and take away ideas to try out in their gardens at home.

'We attract 750,000 visitors annually to the shows we produce,' explains Bob Sweet, Head of Shows Development for the RHS. 'People have different expectations of each. At Chelsea the emphasis is on quality, glitz and glamour, and fashion features very highly, while at Hampton Court we focus on innovation, and we're developing a grow-your-own theme at the moment. And Tatton has regional craftspeople, such as stonemasons. Hampton Court is the

largest show, attracting up to 185,000 people. But some, such as the London Orchid Show, are quite tiny, attended by just 5000 or 6000 people. This is highly specialist, and the people who attend are willing to travel a very long way to see what orchids we have.'

The Society's Shows department has four sections: Development, Operations, Special Events and Administration. Each plays its part in putting on the shows, but it is Development that manages the horticultural side of things and decides which categories of garden exhibits to include (such as Chic or Courtyard), works out where the show gardens will be located, chooses which designers to feature and coordinates the trade stands and media coverage. Bob oversees the 16 Show Managers who work in the

ABOVE LEFT *Enthusiasts come from afar to see orchids exhibited*

OPPOSITE *Trevor Tooth's 'Love, Life and Regeneration' garden at the 2006 Hampton Court Palace Flower Show contained a steel 'story den' as a space for reflection*

Development team. All are experienced horticulturists, as part of their role involves designing and developing garden features. For example, Tatton Park hosts the National Flower Bed Competition, where local authorities compete to plant beds excelling in quality, design and innovation. And the 2007 BBC Gardeners' World Live featured a display of National Plant Collections, developed with the National Council for the Conservation of Plants and Gardens (NCCPG). Planning begins more than a year in advance, with the Development team discussing the look and feel of the show, inviting applications from exhibitors and working out the judging criteria. 'Back in early 2007, Chelsea's Show Manager, Alex Baulkwill, was already developing the idea of featuring organic edible plants at the 2008 show,' says Bob.

Birth of the annual flower show

Flowers and vegetables were exhibited at Horticultural Society meetings as far back as 1805, when a Mr Minier brought with him a new variety of potato for examination by the Fellows. Then, in 1827, the Society decided to host a public breakfast at its Chiswick garden in place of its annual anniversary dinner. The fête was a great success, and the phenomenon of the annual flower show was born. In 1829 *The Times* reported of the event: 'It forms one of the principal attractions of the fashionable season, and is looked forward to with more anxiety than any other fête, either public or private.'

On one occasion visitors' carriages extended from the entrance of Kensington to Turnham Green, more than 3 km (2 miles). In 1831, the Horticultural Society introduced competitive classes in the hope they would stoke up interest in its meetings and encourage more visitors through the gates of its shows. It decided to award Banksian medals (named after RHS founder Sir Joseph Banks) for the best displays of rhododendrons, azaleas, grapes, roses, melons, pineapples, dahlias and camellias at meetings and shows held throughout the horticultural year. The tradition of awarding medals at its shows has continued ever since (see Reaping rewards, pp. 90–91).

The grounds of Chelsea Hospital were first used to host a major flower show in 1912 and, for garden and floral designers, gaining a Gold medal at Chelsea is now the ultimate accolade. Many begin planning their exhibits months ahead, carefully honing the schedules to ensure their flowers, vegetables and greenery will be at their best when the judges make their

OPPOSITE ABOVE *An advisory stand at the 1913 Chelsea Flower Show*

OPPOSITE BELOW *Preparing the ground for Chelsea Flower Show in 1936 involved just as much hard work and effort as it does today*

rounds on the first afternoon. Exhibitors from overseas quite often participate as a means of attracting tourists and increasing awareness of their natural environments. Having to fly in plants from thousands of miles away means they have an even greater task of ensuring the blooms reach the show in tip-top condition.

One such exhibitor is Suzanne Gaywood, who has created a floral exhibit representing Grenada, her home country, since 1998. Each year she visits the country around Christmas time and meets with growers to discuss what plants she needs and who will be able to supply them.

'I go round the gardens and identify what I want to use,' she explains. 'I have an idea in my head at that point about what the exhibit will look like. However, it's very much subject to availability. We have certain things against

ABOVE *In the Great Pavilion, boxes of flowers and foliage are gradually unpacked during the build-up to opening day at the Chelsea Flower Show*

us – for example, Mother's Day is very big in Grenada and is in the second week in May. This means anthuriums and orchids and other smaller flowers are very much in demand. And this year, 2007, we've had the Cricket World Cup to contend with because hotels wanted extra flower arrangements to impress the visitors.'

Suzanne came to the UK when she was in her late teens to train as a hairdresser. She built up her own business but sold it after getting married and having her first daughter. Arranging flowers became a means of occupying herself. 'I feel it was a fortunate accident that I made the decision to sell my business and then diverted to floral design as a means of amusing myself,' she says. 'That was in 1986. In 1989 I was invited to assist at the first-ever Chelsea exhibit from the Windward Islands, covering St Lucia, St Vincent, Dominica and Grenada. I did that for one day and then was asked back again the following year.' This time Suzanne was there for three days and was more involved in the flower arranging. Eventually she saw the opportunity for exhibiting solely for Grenada.

'I felt Grenada would benefit from having its own exhibit advertising itself as the Isle of Spice,' she says.

'I go round the gardens and identify what I want to use. I have an idea in my head at that point about what the exhibit will look like. However, it's very much subject to availability.'

'After a while of kicking around Chelsea doing lots of interpretive designs and flower arranging, the show manager began inviting me to exhibit in the Great Marquee. As an individual, without the backing of a horticultural society, I was a little bit daunted by the prospect but eventually agreed to do it. At the time, I didn't even know how much funding I needed – I was completely at sea. I approached the High Commissioner of Grenada, who was fortunately a very keen plantswoman, and she took it upon herself to find the sponsors.'

Suzanne set about finding a team of people who could help her meet the exacting demands of a Chelsea exhibit. In Grenada she recruited four growers, including estate owner and entrepreneur Denis Noel OBE, nursery owner John Criswick, president of the Orchid Circle of Grenada Cathy John and proprietor of Bay Gardens in Grenada, Albert St Bernard. At home, she enlisted the help of her husband and several willing neighbours: Brian and Sue Cumming, Dave and Jane Weedon, plus Ivor and Gill Brearley. Her first

exhibit, entitled 'Grenada, Isle of Spice', won Silver in 1998. Following this initial success, Suzanne went on to win Silver-Gilt in 1999, 2000 and 2006 plus Gold in 2001, 2002, 2003, 2004 and 2005. In 2006 she was invited to attend the Women of the Year lunch in recognition of her outstanding achievements in the field of floral design and for successfully competing with exhibits run by companies with much larger teams and budgets. Although sponsors such as the Grenada Board of Tourism, the Horticultural Society of Grenada and British Airways have helped push up her budget over the years, her operation is still relatively small compared with some of the other entrants.

'In the early days we had to cut corners – we couldn't afford hotel accommodation; we had to stay with friends and family. But getting Silver that first year encouraged us to go on. We've since got more demanding and adventurous with our designs, so it costs us more now, but it's still very modest. The reason is that my neighbours lend their time and talent for free.'

ABOVE *Suzanne Gaywood sits beside her floral exhibit 'Time & Tide'*
at the 2007 Chelsea Flower Show

Going for gold at Chelsea: 'Time & Tide'

On a hot day in late April 2007, Suzanne shows off the embryonic structure of the exhibit she is planning to take to the 2007 Chelsea Flower Show. Sitting in the back garden of her neighbour's house in the village of Woodham Walter is a small shelter, with a rusting corrugated-iron roof, and a newly constructed wooden platform. The theme of the garden is to be 'Time & Tide', with the structure destined to become an old fisherman's shelter and rotting jetty. The prop has been created by Brian Cumming. He has built all Suzanne's structures to date, with help from Suzanne's husband, Peter, Dave Weedon and Ivor Brearley. They range from a water wheel and sugar factory to a ruined church and a mountain plus waterfall. Suzanne plans to 'age' this year's creation by staining it with coffee and earth.

'Last year's exhibit was very green and had a rainforest theme,' she says. 'This year I want it to look romantic – like a little old bay on a Caribbean island that's been worn away by time and tide and has an abandoned feel to it. I've got some old things, including a lantern and anchor and an old chest to use as props. It may look quite bare at the moment, but I can see the potential.'

Four weeks later, the build-up for Chelsea 2007 is under way. In the open air, fork-lift trucks zip back and forth placing earth, stones and sculptures into the evolving landscapes of the show gardens. Film crews zoom in on the anxious faces of designers directing where bamboos and olive trees should be planted, while tradesmen set up stalls selling everything from plant labels to designer furniture and large pieces of driftwood. The interior of the Great Pavilion, successor to the Great Marquee, where Suzanne's 5 sq-m (16 sq-foot) raised plot is located, has the air of a disorganized florist's shop. In the centre, a small forest has sprung up, while across the way a jungle of tree ferns is being assembled. Trolleys stand stacked with pots topped with brown-paper tubes, from which peep perfect gold and burgundy roses. Some exhibits seem close to completion, while others are as yet devoid of vegetation. On one of the more advanced stands, a life-size beaded rhinoceros prowls among a fan of banana leaves.

Amid the organized chaos, Suzanne's derelict fisherman's shelter is quietly coming to life. The 76 boxes of flowers and leaves that arrived from Grenada three days earlier have been unpacked and sorted by type into buckets of

'I get inspiration as I go along. If something doesn't look right, I just know. Yesterday we had white orchids coming out of the roof. They were spectacular, but every time I looked at them I knew they weren't right.'

water. Stalks of red, yellow and pink heliconias, plastic-covered anthuriums, ornamental bananas, shampoo gingers, philodendron leaves and bromeliads wait beside picture-perfect pots of orchids to be selected. Suzanne is busy arranging them around her props. Beside the jetty on one face of the square exhibit are rusting chains, worn ropes and an old rum barrel representing the Caribbean slave trade. The next face displays a sweep of striking crimson *Heliconia* 'Johnson Beharry VC', a new cultivar that was discovered to have hybridized naturally on Grenada. It was named in 2006 after Grenadian soldier Lance-Corporal Johnson Beharry, who was awarded the Victoria Cross for bravery in Iraq. Delicate cream and pink orchids protrude from an opening in the roof of the shelter, while glowing yellow and red heliconias burst from its dim interior.

'I get inspiration as I go along,' says Suzanne. 'If something doesn't look right, I just know. Yesterday we had white orchids coming out of the roof. They were spectacular, but every time I looked at them I knew they weren't right – they stood out too much. I replaced them with cream ones, and that works much better with the rustic nature of the exhibit.' By late afternoon Suzanne is beginning to worry that she may not have enough foliage. Some of the leaves she ordered arrived damaged and so can not be used. 'Sometimes in the past we've had to go and visit the skips to see if anyone's thrown out anything worth having,' she admits. 'I think it's a distinct possibility this year.'

When the day of judging dawns, however, Suzanne's fears have subsided, and she's quietly confident. The stand looks magnificent, each side's theme blending seamlessly into the next through her artistic placement of contrasting colours and textures. A spike of driftwood has been adorned with palm leaves to create a lifelike tree, the weathered jetty is decked with anthuriums and ornamental *Musa* and the elegant show of *Heliconia* 'Johnson Beharry VC' now provides the backdrop to a display of the spices for which Grenada is famous: nutmeg (*Myristica fragrans*), turmeric root (*Cucuma longa*), clove (*Syzygium aromaticum*), cinnamon (*Cinnamomum zeylanicum*) and cocoa (*Theobroma cacao*). The whole exhibit is surrounded by sand, making the onlooker feel as though they were standing in the shallows just offshore. Mellow rhythms of a live steel band add to the Caribbean island atmosphere. Her hard work over, Suzanne sups a glass of rum punch and eagerly anticipates the judges' decision.

Going for gold at Chelsea: 'A Pleasance for the Rose and Lily Queen'

Outside in the open air, the Garden exhibits, divided into Show, Chic, City, Courtyard and Roof gardens, are by now also finished and pristine. Among the designers awaiting the judges' decisions are two first-time exhibitors at Chelsea, Anthea Guthrie and Alan Gardner. Anthea's exhibit is one of the Courtyard gardens and stands at the end of an avenue of small, square displays. They include 'Shinglesea', a re-creation of the Victorian fashion for using disused railway carriages for seaside holiday homes; 'Le Jardin de Vincent', a botanical interpretation of Vincent van Gogh's paintings created

OPPOSITE *Suzanne's exhibit conjures up the feel of an abandoned fishing jetty, worn by time and tide*

using dark-green cypresses and brightly coloured irises and calendula, and 'Tufa Tea', a celebration of the 1930s habit of taking tea in the garden. Anthea's theme is 'A Pleasance for the Rose and Lily Queen'.

'It's set in 1636,' she says, 'and it's a courtly outdoor theatre for Queen Henrietta Maria, who was the wife of Charles I, the reigning monarch of the time. She was a teenage bride from France who used to act in plays written for her by Ben Jonson, with sets designed by Inigo Jones. I got the inspiration at the Hampton Court Palace Flower Show last year … Henrietta Maria and Charles used to quarrel, and she would run away from him, so, initially, I was going to design a 'running-away' garden. But when I discovered she liked acting I thought I'd create a nice, secret, girly garden for her to act in.'

As Chelsea 2007 gets under way in the drizzling rain, the stage is set for Jonson's *Chloridia* in Anthea's garden exhibit. Her niece Catherine Lindsey, dressed in authentic seventeenth-century costume, is playing the part of Henrietta, who in turn is playing the part of Flora, the goddess of flowers. She sits atop a Welsh oak throne carved in the shape of a lily beneath a specially commissioned iron arch. The backdrop is an Inigo Jones design depicting a woodland glade. In the foreground is a box-edged parterre garden with white 'Winchester Cathedral' roses similar to the kind that would have been available at the time. In an unusual collaboration, these were grown with

ABOVE *Anthea Guthrie's outdoor theatre garden pays homage to Queen Henrietta Maria, wife of Charles I* assistance from inmates at Park Prison in Bridgend, south Wales. As Henrietta was a patron of French garden designer André Mollet, Anthea took the shape of the parterre from a much bigger design of Mollet's. At the front of the symmetrical garden are plantings of gooseberry topiary grafted on to redcurrant stalks. And complementing the fruit trees are royal white lilies, symbolizing the chastity and purity of the royal marriage.

'I came across a book called *Drama at the Courts of Henrietta Maria*, and from that I chose the play,' Anthea explains. 'Then I researched the authentic backdrop, the costume and the kind of ironwork. We created the throne and the arches; they are not a copy from history. But we know that monks experimented with grafting and topiary in the Renaissance.'

Going for gold at Chelsea: 'Perspectum'

While Anthea's Courtyard garden is shrouded in history, Alan Gardner's Chic exhibit, 'Perspectum', is as modern as they come. On the left-hand side of his square plot is an undulating turf, topping a case of clear perspex filled with black cobbles. On the right-hand side, the floor is paved with sleek black tiles at the front and covered in more black pebbles at the back. The exhibit is sliced in two from left to right by a large sheet of Plexiglass, into which Alan has made jagged cuts. These mirror the shape of the leaves of the maple planted behind the screen. The bright lime of the maple contrasts strikingly with the purple beech hedge that forms the rear boundary to the garden. Alan, who wears bright-red nail varnish and sports dyed-blue hair, sees himself very much as an artist rather than a garden designer.

'The garden is meant to be seen in the rain,' he says cheerfully, as the morning's drizzle intensifies into a downpour. 'The garden is divided by a series of Plexiglass panels which the rain runs down, so obscuring the visibility as you go through. I designed it as a picture on the wall, a view through a window, rather than as a useful space. The polished-granite floor is more mirror pool than patio, while the turf wave connects the two spaces, almost as if that Plexiglass screen is a mirror in between, and the rear section of turf reflects the front piece. The Plexiglass that holds the turf wave condenses up in the wet and obscures the contained cobbles, then exposes them again when the weather dries out.'

Alan's interest in creating landscape-based installations dates back to his childhood. Brought up in a suburb of Birmingham, by parents uninterested in gardening, he one day pestered his father to buy him a cactus for his windowsill. Soon Alan was growing fruit and vegetables and installing greenhouses in his parents' back garden. And, by the age of 15, he was exhibiting marigolds at the Birmingham Flower Show. After leaving school Alan ended up working for Birmingham Council's parks division and at 21 was running their central tree nursery, as their youngest-ever propagator. Eventually he left to work for himself, and found work doing mowing, weeding and a little landscaping. By 2001 he had decided to focus on garden design.

'I'd never been trained as a garden designer but I was quite successful,' he says. 'I mostly designed everyday gardens for private individuals. About three or four years ago I came to the conclusion that there had to be an Alan Gardner way of doing things, just as there was a Dan Pearson style and a Christopher Bradley-Hole style. I've since done 23 show gardens, and I've developed a style of my

own. Plants and gardening used to be very important to me, but suddenly, a few years ago, something turned, and I became more excited by the forms and the shapes than by the plants. I'm dyslexic and because of that my spatial awareness is greater than most people's. I tend to see things in 3-D spaces – I can capture something in my head and move around that space. I can't deal with words – I deal with spaces.'

Alan's inspiration for his first-ever Chelsea garden was dictated partly by the size of the plot, a strict 4.5x5 m (15x17 feet). He spent three months working out what he should include in the space. 'I wanted to put something in it that was an installation, something that was really me and that wasn't a cop-out just to be at the Chelsea Flower Show,' he says. 'It had to have some

ABOVE LEFT *Alan Gardner (far left) begins to construct his first Chelsea exhibit*

OPPOSITE *'Perspectum' is a minimalist mix of shape, colour and texture*

land-art, which is the turf shaping, and I wanted to do something that reacted with the environment that it was in. Last year when I was exhibiting at Hampton Court I created a garden with a huge timber frame, which, when you looked through it, enclosed Hampton Court Palace. Here there is nothing to grab, nothing to take, from the surrounding landscape. I wanted to do something that was a picture on the wall – that was not accessible and hadn't got to be practical. I didn't want to get bogged down with furniture and how people would use the space. So I came up with the idea of dividing it up with Plexiglass to capture the rain and change the degree of transparency through the site. It's very difficult to do a garden like that. It's like a naked human being – it shows everything. My fellow exhibitors have the luxury of planting their gardens up with lots of frothy flowers that cover up the paving and break down the edges, but in my garden there is nothing to cover up anything. She's out there as she is.'

Going for gold at Chelsea: judgement day

At some point during the Sunday and Monday, all the exhibitors have to leave their stands to allow the judges to come by and scrutinize their entries. They assess the quality of the design, planting and construction, and consider how the designer has interpreted the theme. Monday evening is a nervous time for competitors, as the results are not announced until the following morning. When the 2007 results are finally revealed, Anthea's and Alan's very first Chelsea entries have both achieved Bronze medals, while old-timer Suzanne has scooped her sixth Gold medal.

'We're thrilled to bits,' she says. 'Trinidad got Gold too, but Jamaica got Silver-Gilt and Barbados got Silver. Last year was disappointing when we got Silver-Gilt after our getting five Gold medals in a row, but it made us sit up and pull our socks up. One of the judges said our flowers look so fresh and vibrant this year that they didn't stay long – the decision was easily made. Someone nominated Gold, someone else seconded it, and that was pretty much that. Earlier today I was interviewed by Rachel de Thame and was on lunchtime TV. Chelsea is such a surreal experience. I'm just a little Essex housewife and a mum then once a year I'm transported to another level of society, meeting the Queen and celebrities.'

After five days, it is time for Suzanne and the other entrants to dismantle their exhibits, for the world's gardening press to withdraw to their offices and

celebrity socialites to move on to the next big event of the summer. But for the RHS Shows staff, the work doesn't end there, as the close of one show simply signals the rapid approach of another. With Chelsea done and dusted, Bob Sweet turns his attention to BBC Gardeners' World Live, Hampton Court and Tatton Park, driven on by the motivation to continue a long tradition of entertaining the public through plants.

'When I worked in landscaping I really wanted to bring pleasure to people who looked at the designs and when I moved into parks I adopted the expression "entertaining people with plants",' he explains. 'I carried that through to the RHS, because I think entertainment is a vital part of what we do in putting on shows, and that it's very important to bring a smile to people's faces. Part of our role is to bring into the shows things that amuse people, things that please them and things that entertain them. At the same time we are there to inspire and educate. You could argue that in many ways we simply provide a day out for people, but if visiting a show heightens someone's interest in gardening or horticulture, or draws their attention to beekeeping or plant conservation, then I believe we are fulfilling our role.'

ABOVE *Exhibits at the shows are designed to inspire and educate, as in this 'Cancer Research UK Garden' by Andy Sturgeon at Chelsea 2007*

OVERLEAF *Landscape architect Robert Myers's Gold-medal winning garden, also at Chelsea Flower Show, 2007*

Reaping rewards

From the outset the Society aimed to reward horticultural excellence. In 1811, it issued its first medal, a gold, commissioned from designer Dr Robert Batty. The front depicted a greenhouse with a legend meaning 'Summer all year round', while the reverse showed the goddess of flowers and the god of gardens. The first recipient was Sir Joseph Banks, for his work as the most active of the Society's founders. Thereafter the medal was called the Banksian and from 1820 was awarded to 'the exhibitors of objects transmitted or brought to the general meetings'.

In 1836, a new medal was struck, which was named the Knightian after Thomas Andrew Knight, the then president. A new hierarchy of gold and silver medals was created, whereby a Large medal was awarded to 'remarkably handsome ornamental plants of recent introduction'; the Knightian for 'specimens of eatable fruits and of ornamental stove or green-house plants'; the Banksian for 'specimens of the ornamental hardy plants, and for culinary vegetables'. In the minutes of its meeting of 16 April 1836 the Council declared that its object

> *has not been to excite at these meetings a spirit of rivalry among the exhibitors, by giving medals to the best only of those whose specimens may have been placed before the Society, but, on the contrary, to reward merit wherever it has been sufficient to justify such a measure.*

More medals were added to the Society's awards quiver between the 1860s and 1920s. By now medals were struck in gold, silver-gilt, silver and bronze. The Lindley medal, named after John Lindley,

ABOVE *C. H. Curtis (far left), Secretary of the Narcissus Committee between 1903 and 1923, judges daffodils with two breeders*

who worked for the Society for 42 years, initially became the second most valuable of the Society's medals. After 1930, this was awarded for exhibits of educational value or special interest. The Hogg medal, introduced in 1898 to commemorate former Secretary Robert Hogg, was awarded to commendable fruit and vegetable exhibits. While the Grenfell medal, instituted in 1919 in honour of President Lord Grenfell, was used initially for general purposes, then to reward notable pictures and photographs and since 1963 for flower arrangements at the Chelsea Flower Show.

Today, the Gold, Silver-Gilt, Silver and Bronze categories of medals remains. At all RHS shows, Flora medals are awarded to Show Gardens, Small Gardens, Flowers and Ornamental Plants. Hogg medals are given to exhibits of fruit; Knightian medals are awarded to vegetable entries; exhibits of special scientific or educational interest gain Lindley medals; while exhibits of pictures, photographs, floral arrangements and floristry are awarded in the Grenfell medal range. The President's Award is given to exhibitors in the Great Pavilion selected as personal favourites of the RHS President – in 2007, Peter Buckley. In addition there are RHS Floral Design Trophies, RHS Floristry Trophies and RHS Junior Display Trophies. All exhibits are judged using standard criteria. At Chelsea 2007, the judges awarded a total of 69 Gold medals.

ABOVE *The Royal Horticultural Society awards Flora medals for winning gardens at each of its shows*

CHAPTER 4

the plant doctors

Andrew Halstead's office on the first floor of RHS Wisley's Laboratory building is just how you imagine an insect-lover's den might look. Packed shelves contain books such as *British Hoverflies* and *Crop Protection*, a box perched high on a cupboard declares 'wasp's nest', while an inflatable 'Benny the Bug' slumps in the pot of a Swiss cheese plant. On a desk, close to a poster showing New Zealand and Australian flatworms, captive tiger-striped cinnabar caterpillars wriggle among ragwort leaves, and humbug-swirled snails glide their way up the vertical walls of a jar. Should any insect prisoners try to escape, an insect net is close at hand. 'I always had a fascination for insects. As a child I used to collect caterpillars in jars and see what they turned into,' says Andrew. 'My father was an ironmonger and kept bees, and I now have three hives that I keep here at Wisley for convenience. I get honey from them most years.'

Andrew is the Royal Horticultural Society's principal entomologist at Wisley. 'It sounds very grand, as though there's a whole army of entomologists here, but in fact it's just me and one other person,' he jokes.

'Much of my work involves identifying specimens that have come in the post. Sometimes they arrive squashed, and you have to use your imagination to work out what they should look like.'

He gained his first degree in 1969 at Nottingham University in the Agricultural Faculty and then later studied for his masters, an MSc in Crop Protection, at the University of Bangor in north Wales. From there in 1972 he went on to join the Royal Horticultural Society as as an entomologist in 1972. RHS members are entitled to free advice on garden pests and diseases and how to handle them, so a large part of Andrew's role is advisory work. Over 3000 queries and samples a year come to him, by letter, phone, e-mail or visitors at shows, all requiring answers. These range from requests to identify mystery beasts that have turned up in someone's garden to the best ways of dealing with common pests such as slugs, and advice on encouraging wildlife into gardens.

'Any enquiry of an animal nature is likely to end up here,' he says. 'Much of my work involves identifying specimens that have come in the post. Sometimes they arrive squashed, and you have to use your imagination to work out what they should look like. And other times people describe the most amazing beast over the phone and when it turns up it's nothing like that.'

OPPOSITE *Wisley's Laboratory building is home to entomologists, botanists, plant pathologists, soil scientists, plant-trials staff and the Herbarium*

Know your pest

In terms of pests with which RHS members most frequently request help, slugs and snails feature regularly, along with the lily beetle, red spider mite and various aphids. The vine weevil (*Otiorhynchus sulcatus*), too, is becoming increasingly troublesome. When adult, this appears as an 8-mm (½-inch) long, dull black beetle with a pear-shaped body. It feeds on the foliage of many herbaceous plants and shrubs, especially rhododendron, evergreen euonymus, hydrangea, epimedium or barrenwort, bergenia, primula and strawberry. Though the adults cause unsightly damage to leaves, it is the fat, white grubs that are more of a problem. These feed on roots and bore into tubers, often killing the plants in the process. The vine weevil has become more prevalent in recent years, partly because of changes in production methods. Whereas nurseries used to grow plants in open fields, they now raise them in pots, creating perfect conditions for weevils. The trend for patio containers may also have contributed to their success. 'The vine weevil has become very much more troublesome over the last thirty to forty years, particularly on plants grown in pots and in other containers,' says Andrew.

Several pests not previously seen in Britain have been noted, thanks to the sharp eyes of RHS members. These include the horse chestnut leaf-mining moth (*Cameraria ohridella*), which was first detected in 2002 as the result of a sample sent in from a garden in Wimbledon. It is now a major problem throughout much of England and is prevalent on all the vulnerable horse chestnuts at Wisley. You can see its impact on the common horse chestnuts in the Pinetum and Arboretum. Where the caterpillars have fed inside the leaves and eaten out the internal tissue, the leaves are coloured with brown blotches. Because the moth has several generations, the damage builds up over the summer months. 'If you have a heavy infestation by the time you get around to late July and August virtually all the leaves have gone brown because it's such a voracious beast, and it is breeding unchecked,' says Andrew.

'It came over to Europe in 1985, into Macedonia, as an undescribed species and later spread to England. No one had seen it before. We still don't know where it came from, although the theory is that it's from somewhere in Asia. It was accidentally introduced, perhaps on imported plants. Because it's come into a new continent, where it hasn't got any effective natural enemies, it is breeding almost exponentially. This is why we are getting such damaging infestations.' Because the damage looks unsightly, it could have an effect in the long term on the trees planted in this country – the common horse chestnut might not be so common in the future.

'The vine weevil has become very much more troublesome over the last thirty to forty years, particularly on plants grown in pots and in other containers.'

Another insect that made its British début through the RHS members' Advisory Service is the berberis sawfly (*Arge berberidis*). This blue-black sawfly was first confirmed as being present in Britain when an adult female was sent to the Advisory Service in April 2002. It was found in a private garden at Church Langley, Essex, where several *Berberis thunbergii* plants had been stripped of their leaves the previous year. Other reports from close to London came to light during 2002, and it soon became clear that severe leaf loss on berberis had been affecting some gardens since at least 2000. As no other insects are known to defoliate berberis, it is likely the sawfly entered Britain in the late 1990s. Andrew has been able to track the pest's subsequent spread

OPPOSITE *Rhododendrons, such as these at Harlow Carr, are a favourite food of the adult vine weevel, which likes to feed on the foliage*

by mapping the distribution of records sent in by RHS members. Initially, it made slow but steady progress from the original area of infestation in the counties around London, but by 2004 there were a couple of more distant records near Lacock in Wiltshire and Dover in Kent. It is possible that these may have resulted from the movement of infested plants, rather than from adult sawflies flying further afield. By the end of 2006, berberis sawfly had consolidated its presence in southeast England and has now been found in the Southampton, Bristol, Coventry, Manchester and York districts.

Berberis sawfly is widely distributed on the mainland of Europe but it has been spreading northwards in recent years. It probably came to Britain with imported nursery stock. The implication is that the warmer temperatures we are experiencing because of climate change have allowed the sawfly to colonize further north and to survive in Britain. Other new insect arrivals likely to have been encouraged by the warmer climes are the rosemary and lily beetles. The rosemary beetle (*Chrysolina americana*), an attractive metallic insect with purple and green stripes, was first reported on rosemary plants in the UK at Wisley in May 1994. Although this population died out, by 1998 reports were coming through of established colonies of the beetle in southeast England,

ABOVE *Plants of* Berberis thunbergii *have been affected by the berberis sawfly, which is extending its range in the UK*

including one near London's Waterloo Station and another in Winnersh, near Reading. A year later, the first enquiry concerning the beetle was received by the Advisory Service, from near Weybridge in Surrey. By the end of 2005, it had become widespread in the London area and is now spreading quite rapidly throughout England. The beetle thrives on rosemary (*Rosmarinus officinalis*) or lavender (*Lavandula* species) but can also feed on thyme (*Thymus* species), sage (*Salvia* species) or Russian sage (*Perovskia atriplicifolia*).

'The rosemary beetle is a Mediterranean insect that is probably here now because we're getting such mild winters,' says Andrew. 'Other pests that are showing the effects of climate change are those that have traditionally been here as glasshouse pests, unable to survive outside. Some are now thriving outdoors in sheltered places. For example, fluted scale and glasshouse thrips are now established out of doors, especially in central London.'

If you've ever seen your beautiful lilies reduced to chewed stumps in a matter of days, the chances are you've had a visit from the scarlet lily beetle (*Lilioceris lilii*). This pest was accidentally imported to the country on several

ABOVE *The lily beetle is now well established in most English counties and parts of Scotland and Ireland*

occasions towards the end of the nineteenth century, but the first established colony was discovered only in 1939 at Chobham, Surrey, by the RHS's first entomologist, George Fox Wilson. An analysis of records held by the Entomology section of the RHS up to 1989, together with the results of an appeal for records of the beetle in the RHS's *The Garden* magazine in 1990, indicated that the beetle's range had extended into Hampshire, Middlesex, Wiltshire, Dorset, Hertfordshire and Oxfordshire. By the end of 2006, the pest had turned up in almost every English county as well as in Glasgow and Belfast.

'The lily beetle was here long before people worried about climate change, and its distribution extends from Europe to China, so it covers quite a lot of climatic zones,' explains Andrew. 'Having said that, during the 1940s to 1960s it was very localized – it was in Surrey and the surrounding counties, but the rest of the country never saw it. It has rapidly increased its spread over the period when we have had very hot, sunny summers, so there may be some climate-change effect there. But it's often very difficult to separate out the influence of climate change from other factors.' Andrew Salisbury, the other entomologist at Wisley, is carrying out research to discover which chemical odours are responsible for attracting the lily beetle to its host plants and parasitic insects to the lily beetle's grubs.

Friend or foe?

As a demonstration garden, Wisley gets the full range of pests that you might expect to find in British gardens, from mammals, birds and insects to mites, molluscs and nematodes. The RHS entomologists have built up considerable knowledge about such pests over the years, and regularly share this with members by holding workshops and garden tours. Knowing about a pest's life cycle can help gardeners target invaders effectively while keeping the use of chemicals to a minimum. A good example is the codling moth (*Cydia pomonella*), which, during its caterpillar stage, eats into apple and pear fruits. If you visit the orchards at Wisley, you might see small open-sided traps hanging in some of the trees. These are pheromone traps that attract the male codling moths to them.

'The trap is based on the chemical that the virgin female codling moth produces as a means of attracting males,' says Andrew Halstead. 'You have an open-sided box with a sticky sheet in the bottom, in the middle of which

OPPOSITE ABOVE *This trap uses pheromones to attract male codling moths*

OPPOSITE BELOW *Codling moths affect fruit trees including apples, pears and crab apples*

sits a pellet that exudes this volatile chemical. When a male codling moth is flying around and sniffs this scent on the wind, it thinks, Yippee!, and dives into the box, only to get stuck. The traps are designed as monitoring devices. You can see when the moths are around because you start catching them, and by counting how many you get a week you can decide whether or not to spray.'

Andrew is keen to point out that not all insects that appear in our gardens are baddies. Many, such as ladybirds, hoverfly lavae, ground beetles and parasitic wasps, play a useful role in eating pests such as aphids, while bees help pollinate plants. In recent years, the RHS has begun promoting the development of wildlife-friendly gardens that encourage a wide range of insects, birds and other animals to them. Actions that can be taken to encourage wildlife include providing nesting boxes for birds, bats and bees, creating a pond, leaving log-piles for insects to live in and allowing grass to remain long at certain times of the year. From the gardener's point of view, the key to good wildlife gardening is to get a balance between the creatures that you don't want and the helpful ones.

ABOVE *Ladybirds are welcome visitors that feed on aphids*

OPPOSITE *Installing bat boxes, bee nests and log-piles in your garden can help attract wildlife*

'The RHS is promoting gardens as places for biodiversity,' says Andrew. 'By doing certain environmentally friendly things you can improve your garden as a wildlife habitat without turning it into a weed patch. However, the best way to encourage good wildlife is to encourage the pests they feed on – you can't have ladybirds without some greenfly, for example. You have to compromise to a certain extent because you can't have lots of beneficial insects and no pests. This is where knowledge comes in. If you can recognize problem pests and tell when they are approaching the stage when they might cause damage, that can help you limit the amount of pesticides you use. For example, some pests don't turn up until the end of the growing season. By that time it doesn't really matter because they're not going to have a big impact on the plant at that time. But if you have a pest in late spring or early summer when the plant is still developing, the impact is going to be much greater.'

Garden doctor

In addition to pests, plant diseases can pose problems for gardeners. Knowledge is useful here too, but identifying what is causing a plant to be sick can be much harder than simply spotting a particular insect. Such is the complexity of some pathogens that even the RHS's pathology experts can have a tricky time identifying them. As a result, the RHS's members' Advisory Service receives around 6000 queries a year about mystery plant illnesses, double the number of queries pertaining to pests. The RHS's principal plant pathologist, Béatrice Henricot, has the job of trying to identify the diseases afflicting samples that members send her. She uses scientific techniques ranging from visual analysis of symptoms to DNA sequencing.

'We have two plant pathologists here, along with a research assistant. People send us everything from a little leaf sample to a whole tree. That yew tree is waiting for a phytophthora test,' she says, pointing to a brown, withered bush standing on one of the desks in her laboratory, awaiting this test for fungal disease. 'And here we have some hostas and lavender samples that have just come in. Usually the pathogens infecting samples are quite common, but sometimes we find new diseases, which can be very exciting.'

Béatrice's most interesting discovery was box blight. In late 1994, a new disease discovered on box (*Buxus*) plants at a nursery in Hampshire was identified as *Cylindrocladium scoparium*, a pathogen that causes disease on a range of hosts. A few years later, symptoms of leaf and twig blight were reported on *Buxus* in New Zealand and identified as being caused by *C. spathulatum* or *C. ilicicola*. When Béatrice received samples of *Buxus* showing similar symptoms in 1998, she realized that, in fact, the species causing the disease was entirely new. Using traditional cultural techniques and DNA sequencing, she described its characteristics and named it *Cylindrocladium buxicola*, after its host plant. When the fungus infects a plant it generates leaf spots that are either dark brown or light brown with a darker rim. It can also cause black streaks on stems. Eventually, the infected leaves die off, and the young plants die. Since the discovery, the blight has become widespread in the UK. So far it has been recorded on three species – *Buxus sempervirens*, *B. microphylla* and *B. sinica* var. *insularis* – plus many of their cultivars. In 2000, it showed up on Box Hill in Surrey, the only major UK location where *Buxus sempervirens* grows wild. Box is one of the oldest species

ABOVE *These* Armillaria *infection trials are designed to help understand that common garden problem, honey fungus*

OVERLEAF *Box parterres, such as this one at Hampton Court Palace, are at risk of being damaged or destroyed by box blight*

of ornamental plants and is a feature of many historic gardens with topiary and box parterres, such as those on display at Hampton Court Palace. 'We're currently undertaking trials to find a fungicide to control box blight,' says Béatrice. 'This project started in 2006 and will finish in 2007 or 2008. We received some funding from English Heritage because they are concerned about its impact on historic gardens. We have it here at Wisley, too.'

Béatrice is also involved with research projects into other diseases that RHS members encounter. These include honey fungus, rusts and powdery mildews. Honey fungus, *Armillaria mellea*, is the most commonly reported disease and

ABOVE *Yew and box hedges are susceptible to diseases, such as phytophthora and box blight*

fortunately is quite easy to identify. It causes trees, shrubs, other woody plants and sometimes herbaceous perennials to die back; often leaves become discoloured and wilt, and sometimes they simply fail to appear in spring. 'If you look at this root, you can see a white layer just under the surface – you have to check the roots,' she says. Another distinguishing feature is the appearance of black bootlace-like strands. These are rhizomorphs that help the fungus travel from plant to plant through the ground.

'You can see them here in this sample,' Béatrice says, taking down a test tube from a cupboard marked 'Honey Fungus Cultures'. The tube contains a thick, brown substance, in which the stringy, black rhizomorphs are clearly visible. Other common diseases that are quite easy to spot are powdery mildews and rusts, and these tend to be host-specific. But other infections can give Béatrice quite a headache. 'I'm not certain yet what has caused this,' she says, pointing to the brown, shrivelled needles on a branch of pine that has come in from Diss in Norfolk. 'It has three potential pathogens on it: *Pestalotiopsis*, which you often find on stressed plants, *Sphaeropsis sapinea*, which causes leaf blight, and a species of *Lophodermium*, which causes needle drop. I think the second one is probably the cause.'

'Finding new hosts and species is always exciting. Uncovering new ways to get rid of them can be a challenge. … There are always things to discover.'

Cases of phytophthora also often require some complex detective work. This group of fungi kills many trees and shrubs. *Phytophthora* species can attack either above or below ground, causing crown and root rots. There are around 80 species of *Phytophthora* around the world, with some 30 present in the UK. However, new ones are being discovered all the time. *Phytophthora infestans* causes potato blight, while *Phytophthora ramorum* is responsible for sudden oak death. Discovered in 1993, the latter is of such concern that RHS staff have to report any cases of it to government plant inspectors, who take samples for evaluation at the Central Science Laboratory in York. The fungus is a worry because it has recently killed large numbers of oaks along the California coast of the USA and is virtually identical to one that attacks rhododendron and viburnum across part of Europe. The fear is that it could start attacking oaks here too. 'We've had cases of it here at Wisley twice,' says Béatrice. 'The first time was five years ago, and then we had it again this year.

It does not appear to attack British oak trees, although it does sometimes infect beech.'

When Béatrice receives a sample that she suspects to be infected with *Phytophthora*, she begins her investigation by trying to grow the fungus in an apple. This is called 'baiting' out the fungus. In an incubator close to her main laboratory, she has shelves of cling-film-wrapped apples, discoloured brown to a lesser or greater extent with her deliberate infections. 'The brown part often becomes quite hard, if *Phytophthora* is present,' she says. She then takes the fungus and grows it on a jelly called agar, before transferring it to water. As a water-borne fungus, it then releases its spores, enabling Béatrice to identify the species using DNA sequencing. The complete process can take several weeks. Around 20–30 per cent of the 300 tests carried out per year in response to members' enquires are positive. This suggests that *Phytophthora* pathogens are among the most frequent causes of plant death in gardens, particularly of woody plants such as yew.

'Sometimes we find an interesting new host for that species, and we have to isolate the fungus, identify it and re-infect the host to prove that our identification is correct,' Béatrice says. 'Finding new hosts and species is always exciting. Uncovering ways to get rid of them can be a challenge, but the more we know, the easier it is to find methods for dealing with the problem. There are always things to discover.'

ABOVE *Armillaria cultures (left) and a mulch trial (right)*

OPPOSITE *Britain's horse chestnut trees are under attack from the leaf-mining moth* Cameraria ohridella

Battle of the bugs and pests

Slugs and snails (various species)

These well-known and much reviled pests are most active from early spring to autumn, when they feed on a wide range of plants. Seedlings and the emerging shoots and foliage of herbaceous plants are particularly vulnerable to their voracious appetite.

Control:

- Encourage predators such as thrushes, toads, hedgehogs and ground beetles
- Place traps near vulnerable plants. These can be scooped-out half orange, grapefruit or melon skins, laid cut-side down, or jam jars partially filled with beer and sunk into the soil. Check and empty them regularly
- Transplant sturdy plantlets that have been grown on in pots, rather than young vulnerable seedlings. Protect transplants with plastic-bottle cloches
- One biological control specific to slugs, which has no adverse effect on other types of animal, is the microscopic nematode or eelworm (*Phasmarhabditis hermaphrodita*). This is watered into the soil. The nematodes enter slugs' bodies and infect them with bacteria that cause a fatal disease

Lily beetle (*Lilioceris lilii*)

This beetle is a voracious pest of lilies (*Lilium* species) and fritillaries (*Fritillaria* species), with both the larvae and adult beetles devouring the foliage during spring and summer. Lily beetle is continuing to spread, although it remains a localized problem in Scotland, Wales and Northern Ireland.

Control:

- Inspect plants regularly, and pick off and destroy any adults, eggs or grubs when seen

Vine weevil (*Otiorhynchus sulcatus*)

Vine weevil causes problems on a wide range of plants, in both its adult and larval stages. The adult beetles chew irregular notches along leaf edges, while the more damaging grubs destroy the roots and tubers of many plants, especially those grown in pots or other containers.

Control:

- On mild evenings, inspect plants and walls by torchlight and pick off the adult weevils. Shake shrubs over an upturned umbrella to collect more. In glasshouses, look under pots and benches where beetles might hide during the day
- Encourage natural enemies. Vine weevils and their grubs are eaten by birds, frogs, toads, shrews, hedgehogs and predatory ground beetles
- A biological control of the larvae is available as a microscopic pathogenic nematode (*Steinernema kraussei*). This should be applied in August or early September when the soil temperature is warm. It works best in moist, open potting composts such as peat or coir

LEFT *Snails are partial to the emerging shoots and foliage of herbaceous plants*

Rosemary beetle (*Chrysolina americana*)

This pest of rosemary, lavender, thyme and sage is a relative newcomer to the UK but is becoming increasingly widespread. The larvae and adult beetles feed on the foliage during August to June. You might find non-feeding adult beetles resting on the plants during the summer.

Control:

- Hand picking can help to keep infestations below the level at which serious damage occurs. With the taller forms of rosemary and lavender, collect the beetles and larvae by tapping or shaking the branches over paper spread beneath the plant

Grey squirrel (*Sciurus carolinensis*)

The agility and ingenuity that grey squirrels employ to obtain food wins them many admirers, but they can be highly destructive. The damage they cause includes eating ripening fruits, flower buds and shoot tips, digging holes in lawns, robbing bird feeders, invading roof spaces, destroying bulbs and corms, and severely damaging young trees through bark stripping.

Control:

- It is not possible to stop squirrels from coming into a garden. Placing wire netting over plants that are being damaged may be of some help. Animal-repellent substances and scaring devices are likely to provide only short-term protection

This is an abridged version of the RHS's 2005 Pest Chart, compiled by Andrew Halstead from enquiries received at the RHS Members' Advisory Service.

ABOVE *Grey squirrels are adept at robbing nuts from bird feeders*

RHS GARDEN TOUR **HARLOW CARR**
with Curator Matthew Wilson

"Inspirational gardening with respect for the environment"

The Royal Horticultural Society acquired Harlow Carr garden in 2001 after merging with the Northern Horticultural Society (NHS). Founded in 1946, the NHS had opened the garden in 1950 on 10.5 ha (26 acres) of woodland, pasture and arable land leased from Harrogate Council. Its aim was to promote and develop 'the science, art and practice of horticulture with special reference to the conditions pertaining to the north of England'. Today, extended to 27.5 ha (68 acres), the garden's location in a wooded Yorkshire valley some 190 m (620 feet) above sea-level provides conditions for a totally different range of plants from the other RHS gardens.

'We can grow North American prairie plants and Sino-Himalayan plants here that wouldn't grow so well at Hyde Hall because it's not wet enough, nor at Wisley because the soil drains like a sieve,' says Curator and Head of Site Matthew Wilson. 'There's an under-layer of heavy clay here with a decent silt clay loam above it, and in some parts of the garden the soil is very acidic, with pH as low as 4.7 in places. As a result we have an amazing collection of rhododendrons. Himalayan blue poppies and primulas grow like weeds. They both hybridize naturally – we've even got our own specific primula hybrid called the Harlow Carr hybrid, which exhibits the most extraordinary dolly-mixture range of colours.'

Matthew was surrounded by plants from a young age, having grown up on a cut-flower nursery owned by his parents. However, he dabbled with a number of careers – including lead singer of an indie band, working as a meat porter and freelancing as a journalist for the *Sun* – before deciding to reconnect with his horticultural roots. After taking a course in amenity horticulture at Hadlow College in Kent, he worked in a public garden in Hertfordshire, then at Hever Castle, Kent, before becoming the Royal Horticultural Society's youngest curator, of Hyde Hall, aged 32. In February 2004 he accepted the challenge of developing Harlow Carr as the RHS's most northerly demonstration garden.

Since stepping into the role, Matthew has begun redesigning the garden from scratch. With 12 million people within a one-hour drive, he has his work cut out trying to create a garden that will appeal to the widest-possible section of the community. His main aim is to help visitors, many of whom are city dwellers, to make a connection with the natural world. 'Our ethos is to promote inspirational gardening with respect for the environment,' he says. 'It's about showing people what they can do without being detrimental to the environment.'

If you stroll northwest from the visitor centre you soon come to the Broadwalk, a wide, grassy slope that leads roughly south between borders, where round-headed purple alliums stand to attention among salvias, campanulas and spiky cushions of ornamental grasses. Matthew reworked

OPPOSITE *Harlow Carr's Broadwalk is packed with perennials*

the original island beds into continuous borders and introduced 5000 new plants, carefully selecting 'naturalistic perennials' that would support each other and be tough enough to withstand drought. Apart from when they were planted, they have never been watered. Now hot dark, spicy colours at the top of the hill slowly give way to silvers, pale blues and whites, naturally drawing the eye down to the stream that lies in the valley bottom and the woodland beyond.

The stream is a natural watercourse that flows through Harlow Carr. If you follow its course right, past thriving clumps of bog arum, moisture-loving Japanese hostas and unfurling bronze leaves of *Rodgersia aesculifolia*, you come to an opening in which stands a single-storey building of creamy Yorkshire stone. This building is of historic significance, having been the very first Harrogate spa bath house; beyond it, just outside the garden, is the hotel set up to serve the spa visitors. 'The spa building is now a study centre,' says Matthew. 'We have some big ambitions for education at Harlow Carr. We're going to build a new £2.6-million sustainable learning centre, which should increase our educational output fourfold.'

Matthew is keen to teach all visitors about environmental issues. No pesticides are used in the garden, fertilizer use is kept to a minimum, and there is no irrigation system. You can witness the benefits of letting nature take its course in the meadow beyond the study centre. From scrutinizing the record books, Matthew's team have concluded that the land has been used as pasture for 200 years. As a result it's amazingly diverse, with some 3000 terrestrial orchids. 'This all used to be close-mown with a gang mower and then someone noticed a few orchids and stopped mowing,' he says. 'It just goes to show what can stay in the seed bed.'

A short stroll from the meadow, beside a clipped evergreen hedge, Matthew is sowing more cornfield annuals such as field poppy and cornflower to create a 'sea of colour' for a new nautical feature. Woven from willow, by Cumbrian basket-maker Phil Bradley, are a pirate ship, complete with Douglas fir mast, a frolicking mermaid and several whales. Having enjoyed his own country upbringing,

Matthew is keen to encourage children to integrate with the environment by playing in the garden. In the woods across the stream there is a Log-Ness Monster built from old tree trunks, along with bivouacs and a fern-roofed shelter. 'I'm a strong believer that you need to engage children,' says Matthew. 'There are lots of opportunities here for them to get involved, rather than ghettoizing them in an adventure playground. We don't have any limitations on picnics, and we don't mind toddlers running around with footballs – because, ultimately, if a plant can't take a two year old kicking a ball at it, it's not much cop.'

On the other side of the hedge from the pirates, rectangular beds cut into a neatly manicured lawn demonstrate that gardening doesn't have to be

ABOVE *Features such as the Log-Ness Monster help children integrate with the natural environment*

islands created by a double-helix planting of the grasses *Panicum virgatum* 'Warrior' and 'Heavy Metal', and mauve-blossomed *Verbena bonariensis*. 'It's 60 per cent roses and 40 per cent grasses, perennials, bulbs and shrubs,' explains Matthew. 'By not growing them as a monoculture we have far fewer pests and diseases. If you put roses all together it's like a TB ward.'

Companion planting is also put to good use in the Kitchen Garden that lies close to the rose borders. Here, in raised beds, lettuce, parsley, chives and perpetual spinach grow alongside the marigolds that help ward off aphids. And cut flowers such as sweet Williams grow next to purple-sprouting broccoli to provide colour as well as taste for the table. The Kitchen Garden is not limited to basics such as carrots, lettuces and potatoes. One bed contains *Cynara cardunculus*, relative of the globe artichoke and commonly known as a cardoon. Today it is often used ornamentally, but its fountain of silver leaves provides fleshy stalks tasty enough to eat, and it was popular in Victorian times blanched, then eaten like celery. The vegetable plots at Harlow Carr and RHS Garden Rosemoor provided the inspiration for the BBC and RHS TV series *Grow Your Own Veg* that was broadcast in early 2007. 'We're brilliant veg growers here – it's a Yorkshire thing, I think,' boasts Matthew.

Beyond the Kitchen Garden is the *Gardens through Time* exhibit that was created to celebrate the Society's bicentenary in 2004. Here, seven gardens show the changing circumstances, fads and fashions that have shaped the evolution of our gardens during the past 200 years. In the first garden, representing 1804, paths are set 1.2–1.8 m (4–6 feet) wide to allow Regency ladies to walk side by side. The second, mid-Victorian, garden is bursting with exotics introduced to Britain by

expensive. Planted with seeds costing no more than £20, they contain produce such as rhubarb, lettuce, garlic and mint, along with showy spikes of lupins and delphiniums. Containers outside the nearby Alpine House have a similar message: gardening can be as cheap and cheerful as you like. Here, salvaged Armitage-ware toilet seats overflow with *Dianthus nitidus*, and an old pair of boots has a new lease of life as a bed for rockery plants, such as tiny red rosettes of *Sempervivum arachnoideum* or cobweb houseleek. 'If you haven't got a garden, you can still grow small plants,' says Matthew. 'We're looking to maximize the funkiness of Alpines – to make them the really cool plants that people want to grow.'

Old favourites are not forgotten, however. If you complete the circuit back to the visitor centre by heading southeast, you come to Matthew's newly redesigned Rose Revolution border. Here climbers such as *Rosa* 'Breath of Life' ascend striking tetrahelix obelisks, while more grounded varieties such as *R*. 'Buff Beauty' and *R*. 'Complicata' fill

ABOVE LEFT *Gardening can be as small scale as you like*

OPPOSITE *Harlow Carr's* Gardens through Time *exhibit was created to celebrate the RHS's bicentenary in 2004*

explorers and colonialists, while the third represents the 1890s, the golden age of the kitchen garden. Later gardens see the introduction of summer-houses and herbaceous borders, culminating in the garden as outdoor room, a space to be enjoyed by all the family.

Across the stream, on the edge of Harlow Carr's woodland, Matthew is looking to the past for the inspiration for his next addition to the garden. This will be a temperate version of sustainable woodland, planted specifically to provide wood for use in the garden and to educate people about trees and their uses. It is being created as part of the Bettys and Taylors of Harrogate 'Trees for Life' campaign. The company produces Yorkshire Tea and Taylors coffee as well as running the Bettys Café tearoom at Harlow Carr. As a means of giving something back to the communities from which it sources its tea and coffee, the company has been planting trees in Ethiopia, Kenya, India, Indonesia and Brazil that local people can use for cattle fodder, building materials and medicine.

'They are about to plant their three-millionth tree, which will come here as part of our new woodland,' says Matthew. 'We plan to use the woodland to provide natural plant stakes and charcoal as well as timber for benches and buildings. We used woodland in this way 200 years ago, before the Industrial Revolution. Our hope is to re-interpret a very old idea for a modern audience.'

CHAPTER 5

young gardeners

At first glance, the physics laboratory at Writhlington Business and Enterprise Specialist School in Radstock, near Bath, looks much like any other classroom. There are the usual desks with sinks and gas taps, and when the bell goes for break time the room fills with giggling, chattering schoolchildren. A closer look, however, reveals some unusual decorations. The far end wall of the classroom is coloured by a rainbow of silk rosettes, awarded not for excellence in the physical sciences but for horticulture. A wooden shelf unit is crammed with 'grow your own palm tree' kits. And if you peek round the door of teacher Simon Pugh-Jones's adjoining office you'll find jars labelled with the names of orchid species such as *Cymbidium erythraeum* and *Bulbophyllum sulawesii* alongside files marked 'magnets', 'light' and 'sound'.

An after-school gardening club

Simon Pugh-Jones is head of physics, but it is his infectious enthusiasm for orchids that has had the greatest impact at Writhlington. Some 17 years ago he set up an after-school gardening club, making use of a disused glasshouse that stood in the grounds. His love of exotics soon spread to his students, and in no time they were propagating orchids from seed and creating their own hybrids as science experiments. Today, some members of the club are so adept at growing orchids that they regularly give presentations about their experiences, and one has even become a judge for the British Orchid Council.

'I started work at the school just as rural science disappeared from the curriculum and our beautiful greenhouse became empty,' explains Simon. 'I feel at home in greenhouses, so I started an after-school club growing bedding plants and making hanging baskets. Little by little orchids came in, and things really grew from there.'

Today, the 12-m (40-foot) greenhouse is bursting with orchid species, such as cymbidiums, phalaenopsis and dendrobiums. Sliding doors divide it into three sections: hot, warm and cool. The hot section has orchids from tropical climes such as Southeast Asia, Costa Rica and Guatemala, while the cold end contains Himalayan natives, some of which grow naturally under snow for much of the year. On narrow benches, tightly packed pots of the spiky-leaved plants struggle to hold aloft voluptuous pale pink and yellow blooms on

OPPOSITE *Pupils from Writhlington Business and Enterprise Specialist School regularly exhibit orchids at RHS shows, such as this*

slender stems. Yet more specimens hang from pipes above, their thin, grey roots overflowing like straggly, ancient hair. And in the only space left, young epiphyte orchids are just sprouting their first tender green shoots from pieces of bark and cork fixed to partition walls.

'This is *Dendrobium unicum* [an orchid endemic to Thailand, Laos and Burma]. It has lovely orange petals, and it smells quite nice too,' says Luke Lucas, one of the chief growers within the gardening club. 'It would normally grow on a tree, but as we can't have great big trees in here we grow it on a little piece of cork bark. Cork is best because it doesn't rot and will support the plant for many years.'

ABOVE *The London Orchid Show in full swing in the RHS's Art Deco Lawrence Hall in the heart of London's Westminster*

Members of Writhlington's gardening club are regular participants in RHS events. The school first exhibited its botanical specimens at RHS Wisley's Orchids for All exhibition in 2000; now every February sees a contingent of pupils head east to show off their blooms at the London Orchid Show. In 2003, they won their first Silver-Gilt medal at the European Orchid Show in Westminster, and in March 2006 received their first Gold medal at the International Orchid Show. The ultimate accolade came later that same year when they entered the Chelsea Flower Show for the first time and struck Gold there too. The orchids exhibited had all been grown by the students and included many plants raised from seed. Each had a label giving information about its natural habitat, conservation status, cultivation and human stories, such as *Encyclia cochleata* being the national flower of Belize.

'The Chelsea Flower Show comes at a bad time of year for students because they have to take exams, but last year a particular group of students had been all the way through the school and said: "It's our last year, so we want to do Chelsea." So we did it for them,' says Simon.

Green shoots of entrepreneurship

As well as participating in shows, the students grow plants from seed and sell the seedlings with instructions on how to nurture them at outlets such as Hillier Garden Centres, Kew Gardens' shops, the Eden Project and Bicton Park botanical gardens. In nature a single orchid seed pod can contain up to a million seeds, but only one or two will survive and grow into orchids. This is because the seeds are very tiny and, with no food reserves, rely on mycorrhizal fungus to germinate. They soon die if they are not in a perfect spot. In the laboratory next to Simon's physics lab, however, there are food supplies aplenty. Here, the students use a nutrient-rich jelly called agar to coax the seeds into life in glass jars. At any one time, there are hundreds of the jars stacked on floor-to-ceiling shelves, each containing a layer of jelly and green shoots ranging from millimetres to centimetres in size. Two years after the seeds are planted they are big enough to sell in the kits. 'We've got about a billion orchids in here,' jokes Luke.

As a business and enterprise specialist school, Writhlington is keen to encourage entrepreneurship among its pupils. Inspired by the orchid kits, Luke and his friend Ben Stokes created a company called Cockroach to sell the palm-tree kits housed in Simon's lab. The 16 rare palm species on offer range from *Acoelorrhaphe wrightii* (the small, neat Everglades palm) to *Caryota mitis* (the fast-growing clustered fishtail palm) and *Dypsis lastelliana* (the easy-to-grow red neck palm). Each kit contains some moss that swells up when watered, two seeds and a pot, plus instructions. Simon's lab contains a cabinet of nine trophies that have been won by the enterprising Cockroach team for their innovative product.

Luke and his friend Ben Stokes created a company called Cockroach to sell the palm-tree kits housed in Simon's lab. Each kit contains some moss that swells up when watered, two seeds and a pot, plus instructions.

'They made £4000 in the first two months of trading,' says Simon. 'Orchid sales did very well last year because of Chelsea. You're not allowed actually to sell plants there, so we just took people's money and name and address and promised to dispatch the plants later. We came back with well over 1000 orders worth some £7000.'

Money raised through the school's botanical ventures goes to fund several overseas projects, including conservation work at Lankester Botanical Gardens in Costa Rica and Yaxha Orchids in Guatemala. It also subsidizes expeditions abroad so students can study orchids in their natural habitat. In 2000, a group of pupils journeyed to Brazil's cloud forest to carry out scientific research and help rescue a threatened colony of the orchid *Masdevallia infracta*, and in 2004 seven students went to Costa Rica to study epiphytes – plants that grow above the ground surface, using trees or objects for support. More than half of the 20,000 orchid species grow in this way. Thanks to the orchid sales, the trip cost a mere £100 per student. During Easter 2007, Luke and Ben were among three students who went with Simon to Laos, where they explored the forests of the Bolevan Plateau. They identified over 100 orchids in the wild and visited local markets to see where orchids are sold to Thai tourists and the Chinese medicine trade. Simon is now working with locals to set up an orchid-propagation laboratory in the country and train coffee growers to grow orchids in the shade beneath their crops. 'The traders are all very keen to get involved because they can see that the current trade is not sustainable and they have to go further and further to collect the plants,' he says.

Conserving an orchid collection

Luke and Ben have also been putting their botanical expertise to use closer to home. A few miles from the school, down a steep, narrow lane bounded by high walls, is Iford Manor. This grand country house is where architect Harold Peto created his famed Italianate Garden in 1899, based around a series of terraces cut back into the steep hillside. You can explore it today, ascending a long flight of steps on to the Great Terrace and then wandering past fluted columns and Roman tombs to the Cloisters, guarded by thirteenth-century lions, and upwards to the Japanese Garden with its tranquil pool. Elizabeth Cartwright Hignett acquired the manor and garden in 1964 after leaving her ancestral home of Aynhoe Park in Northamptonshire. Together with her husband, she renovated Peto's garden and now opens it to the public on weekday afternoons during the summer.

ABOVE *Ben Stokes (left) and Luke Lucas set up a company selling palm-tree kits*

OVERLEAF *The pair have become expert growers since joining Writhlington's gardening club, tending orchids like these*

'Harold Peto's nephew, Sir Michael Peto, from whom I bought Iford Manor, was a very good gardener,' she says. 'However, he had fallen down a lift shaft at the end of the war and was in a pretty dicey condition for the rest of his life and couldn't do all that much. So the garden had had five years of total neglect. It was in a very bad state and has really taken 35 years to recover.'

It is not the Peto Garden that the Writhlington boys have been helping out with, however. Across from the public garden is Elizabeth's private garden. Here, she has several outdoor 'rooms' including a sloping meadow with a

topiary sofa, chair, table and teapot cleverly fashioned from box and ivy. There are also two glasshouses, one of which is crammed with orchids. Elizabeth brought the collection, gathered by her family over the years, when she moved from Aynhoe. Her gardeners didn't really know what to do with them, so after seeing a Writhlington exhibit at a country show she contacted Simon Pugh-Jones. Luke and Ben spent three days at Iford Manor, splitting and repotting the 80 plants, almost doubling the size of the collection in the process.

'Not many orchids in the UK are old, but Elizabeth has an old collection dating back to the 1800s, and they are quite rare ... We snapped a lot of the bulbs off and repotted them and cleaned them up, and now we maintain them.'

'Not many orchids in the UK are old, but Elizabeth has an old collection dating back to the 1800s, and they are quite rare,' says Luke. 'We went to have a look, and they were in a dire state, in great big china pots that were cracked and rotten. Some were bulging over the top. We snapped a lot of the bulbs off and repotted them and cleaned them up, and now we maintain them for Elizabeth. We go over every couple of months to advise her on how to water and feed them.'

Five generations of Writhlington pupils have now passed through the gardening club. When a pupil has been a member of the club for a year, they are given a family of orchids to look after: Ben is currently in charge of the *Stenoglottis* plants. At 15, Ben and Luke are now two of the most experienced gardening-club members at Writhlington. They plan to stay on for another three years before pursuing horticultural careers. They learnt their orchid-growing skills through former gardening-club members such as Callum Swift and Chris Ashman, who are now both studying botany at university. Today it is Ben's and Luke's turn to act as mentors for the younger gardeners coming into the glasshouse. During break times, they have taken it upon themselves to keep a watchful eye out for footballs kicked by less green-fingered youngsters. 'A ball coming through this glass can do a lot of damage,' says Ben, idly picking up an American football from an assortment of confiscated balls in the glasshouse. 'We get a lot of gyp for nicking their balls, but orchids are more important,' says Luke.

OPPOSITE *Harold Peto's ultra-romantic Italianate Garden at Iford Manor*

In 2007, Ofsted described Writhlington as 'a school with many outstanding features'. It noted that: 'The unusually wide range of businesses run successfully by the students provides an excellent context in which students develop an understanding of global issues and the world of work. There are productive links with companies and organizations across the world.' The gardening club has undoubtedly contributed to the school's success by helping to raise its profile and imbuing students with a sense of pride. And by providing opportunities for its members to give talks, set up companies, win awards and travel to remote rainforests, the club has helped pupils become more articulate, self-confident and worldly wise.

The Flourish campaign and growItcookIt

The RHS aims to enable any UK school to emulate Writhlington through its Campaign for School Gardening, launched in September 2007. The Society is setting up an interactive website to provide resources and encourage teachers to engage pupils in gardening. It plans to give awards to schools as they attain set levels of achievement laid out in a new benchmarking scheme. It is also employing trained horticulturists to work as regional officers and offer hands-on support to participating establishments.

The RHS's Flourish scheme has demonstrated how gardening can help children understand the economic and environmental value of plants, while building up team-working and problem-solving skills. After launching the scheme at Tatton Park Flower Show in 2004, the RHS completed projects in nine schools across the country. These ranged from turning an uninspiring patch of tarmac at Haseltine Primary School in Lewisham, London, into a jungle of palms and ferns complete with pirate ship, to building a multicultural garden at Clapton Girls Technology College in east London, drawing elements from medieval apothecary and formal Islamic gardens. The Society also set up three projects aimed at helping pupils learn about environmental issues through gardening. The first, in Leedstown, Cornwall, created an organic fruit and vegetable garden so pupils could experiment with composting and growing unusual vegetables such as chillies. The second involved building a school allotment at Peover Superior School in Cheshire. This project aimed to rekindle an interest in agriculture among pupils who were largely drawn from

OPPOSITE *Where do fruit and veg come from?*
Help is at hand at Rosemoor

farming families. Meanwhile, the third project helped students in the Midlands create a wild-flower meadow using native species. When it was finished, Birmingham's poet laureate and the Arts Council organized a poetry workshop in the meadow.

In 2005 the RHS expanded its outreach work by joining the 'growItcookIt' project, a Helen Hamlyn Trust initiative. This initially partnered two RHS horticultural project officers with ten schools in the south of England. Once established, it placed two more workers in ten schools in the north of England. The staff visit each school weekly and will maintain contact for three years, training children, teachers and parents. Nicola Wright is one of the outreach workers on the northern scheme. She started her RHS career at Harlow Carr as assistant to Curator and Head of Site Matthew Wilson. Later, she decided she would like to work with children and so undertook a diploma in social and therapeutic horticulture at Askham Bryan College near York.

'I'd seen the benefits horticulture could have when I worked to create a garden with some 14–16-year-old children on a farm. They had been expelled from pretty much every school in Leeds. In their normal, everyday environment they could be a complete nightmare, but when we put them in a gardening situation, where everyone was on a level, it was hard for them not just to focus on gardening and let everything else drift away. From the therapy side of things I think it did those children a lot of good.'

Nicola started work for the Flourish project in 2006. She and her co-worker Sarah-Jane Mason began by assessing each of the schools to locate the sunniest spots for growing vegetables. Some of the schools already had gardening clubs and a handful of tools, but others needed to be equipped from scratch. 'All the schools are completely different,' she says. 'There are two inner-city schools, and a couple that are quite rural. With some, the only suitable space was at the corner of a playing field, making it quite open to the elements, while others have enclosed quads.'

'There are 25 languages spoken in this school. Gardening is a way of communicating at a level everyone can understand.'

Included in the latter category is St Bartholomew's Primary School in Armley, Leeds, that Nicola visits every Thursday. The school is located in a run-down part of the city and bounded by a high metal fence that gives it a drab, prison-like appearance from the outside. On the inside, though, the school is much less gloomy. On one wall of the large classroom in which Nicola is based is a 'tremendous tree', which has multicoloured cut-outs of hands for its leaves. Each one notes a good deed done by one of the pupils, such as 'Anisa created an interesting sculpture out of Play-Doh and sticks' and 'Tyler had some fantastic ideas for his wolf story'. Potted plants sit atop a blue and yellow check tablecloth at the side of the room, and, from the windows, pupils can glimpse the distant hills beyond the city.

Today, the first part of the class involves pupils planting seed potatoes in sturdy plastic bags at one corner of the small quad. By late afternoon, the sun has all but disappeared from the enclosed paved area, but the three raised beds, in which pupils have sowed seeds over the past weeks, are overflowing with healthy-looking plants. There are spiky shoots of onions and spring onions, shiny red-veined leaves of Swiss chard, pink-flowered 'Sugar Ann' peas

OPPOSITE *Gardening can be enjoyed by people of all ages*

and a turquoise tub of 'Pink Panda' strawberries. Nicola deems that the radishes are ready for harvesting, and they all pick some so that the children can taste them. Once they are back inside the classroom and sitting cross-legged in a circle, Nicola washes and slices the bulbous pink and white roots and hands round a plateful of pieces. This is the first crop that the children have planted, nurtured and eaten as part of the northern growItcookIt project. Most of the youngsters, whose nationalities span British, Polish, Slovakian, Indian and Pakistani, take one of the peppery morsels that Nicola proffers and pop it in their mouth. When Nicola asks for a show of hands as to who likes it, at least half the children put up their hands. 'There are 25 languages spoken in this school,' she says. 'Gardening is a way of communicating at a level everyone can understand.'

Ultimately, Nicola hopes the Flourish project will help children to rediscover the link between what they eat and where it comes from. A survey organized by the Linking Environment and Farming (LEAF) organization in June 2007 found that a fifth of Britain's adults did not know that bacon comes from pigs and a third were not aware that oats are grown by British farmers. Around half the population had no idea that hops used to make beer are produced in this country. Earlier in the year, the dairy industry had carried

out a similar survey of 1000 children. One in ten eight-year-olds did not know that pork chops came from pigs, while 18 per cent were left scratching their heads over the ingredients of yoghurt. Pupils of inner-city schools often have the least opportunities for connecting with the natural world.

'I was planting out beetroot seedlings the other day, and one little girl's mum asked, "Where will the beetroot grow and how big will it get?"' recalls Nicola. 'She didn't know how far apart to space the plants. I had to explain that the beetroot we eat is the root part that grows in the ground. You expect people to know things like that, but they just don't. When you buy beetroot in the supermarket it has had its head and tail chopped off, so people don't recognize it as a plant with leaves and roots.'

Nicola also hopes that over time the gardening work undertaken by the pupils will feed into a range of subjects rather than just geography or science. At one school she noted that there was a beautiful carpet of daffodils. However, rather than being asked to go outside and pick the flowers, pupils in an art class were sitting sketching an artificial peony. 'It was gorgeous, but it was completely out of season,' she says. 'It would have made more sense to

me for the pupils to go outside and cut the flowers and learn where they come from and to paint daffodils in March when they are in flower.' Another of the schools she visits has a lot of trees, but few of the pupils had taken the time to look at any of them and were unaware that they had taken some 80 to 100 years to grow. Nicola decided to stimulate the children's interest by getting them to gather leaves so they could study their different shapes. Afterwards she showed them how they could be turned into a mulch to suppress weeds. 'We had a lesson looking at the leaf shapes and trying to work out which tree each one came from,' she says. 'It was a simple thing to do, but it helped them to notice their surroundings and appreciate the different trees. You can fit gardening or horticulture into every single subject in some way.'

Green learning

As well as sending staff into schools to promote gardening, the Royal Horticultural Society welcomes school parties to each of its gardens. Its trained education officers lead themed programmes that complement subjects studied at the various key stages of the National Curriculum. For example, children taking its Tree-mendous Trees tour investigate the influence of mathematics in nature by discussing whether the tallest trees have the widest girth and studying the differing numbers of prickles on holly trees. Those on an Art in the Garden workshop analyse the colours and three-dimensional shapes of plants and gather natural materials with which to create a piece of art. And those on the Poetry and Music workshop are encouraged to use their senses and find suitable words to describe what they discover in the garden.

The Seeds and Growth workshop is a popular option for teachers wanting to explore seeds and how plants grow well. On a hot summer's morning, a crocodile of young children from Pinewood School in Farnborough, Hampshire, winds its way up RHS Wisley's Weather Hill into the Hillside Events Centre to begin the course. As the children sit cross-legged on the floor, munching on apples, Schools Education Officer Judy Moss begins the class by handing round a variety of seeds and pods and asking the four and five year olds what they know about the plants from which they come. First up, a large, smooth coconut fruit and the hairy seed that grows inside it. The children identify it straight away, then learn how the sea helps disperse the seeds when they fall on to the shore.

OPPOSITE *Children from Pinewood School on a visit to Wisley explore where plants come from*

Judy asks a girl in a pink gingham hat to stand up and hold her hand out for some tiny seeds. When she blows on them, they rise up into the air, demonstrating, Judy says, how the wind can also spread seeds far and wide. Next, Judy places a barbed seed on to a ginger-haired boy's T-shirt. After he has energetically jumped up and down, pretending to be a rabbit, she shows the class that the seed is still there, illustrating the role of animals in distributing seeds. Finally, she rattles a seed pod containing Brazil nuts. 'How do you think the nuts get out of this hard case?' she asks. After a few intelligent, but wrong, guesses by the class she holds up a picture of a small furry animal. 'This agouti gets the nuts out of the pods,' she explains, 'but what do you think it uses to do that?' A chorus of 'its teeth' comes back from the children.

Having learnt about the different sizes and shapes of seeds, the children walk to the vegetable garden, pausing *en route* to examine the candle-like seed pods of a large Indian bean tree (*Catalpa bignonioides*). A timber gate leads through a dense hornbeam hedge into the garden, where rows of raised beds are packed with rounded rows of red and green lettuces, spiky garlic leaves, rocket, radishes and other vegetables. The children look at each type of plant

ABOVE *Picking flowers when no one is looking*

and have to say which part of the plant we eat. They recognize that the edible part of carrots grows beneath the soil and that we eat the leaves of lettuce but are flummoxed when confronted by a giant silver-leaved globe artichoke. 'It's this round part here, at the top, that we eat,' explains their teacher, Early Years Manager Jean Ingram. Beside a low wall is a pot spilling over with various types of salad leaves, which the children are invited to taste. 'Mmm, I love lettuce,' says one girl, enthusiastically helping herself to handfuls of the healthy green leaves. 'Ugh, I don't like this,' says another, spitting out a piece of rocket. 'It's making my tongue hot.'

After a short break in the shade of a whitebeam tree, the children visit the fruit garden, where they have to identify all the different ingredients that could make up a fruit salad. Some are quick to spot clusters of shiny redcurrants and plump, pink raspberries, but others clearly can't tell their grapes from their gooseberries. Jean explains that most of the children have two parents out at work and those with one parent at home are usually vying for their attention with younger brothers and sisters and don't often get the opportunity to explore the natural world. 'I'd say that only four or five out of 20 children have any knowledge about fruit, vegetables and flowers and where they come from,' she says. 'That's why we came here today. I wanted to show the children where their fruit and vegetables come from so they have an understanding that it doesn't just come from a supermarket shelf. In this day and age when everyone's talking about sustainability, it's vital that children understand there's not an endless conveyor belt supplying their food.'

ABOVE *Finding out which plants are which*

Learning curve

The Horticultural Society of London (later RHS) first mooted the idea of training gardeners in 1820. It soon began recruiting 'labourer–students', who had to be aged between 18 and 26, unmarried and literate. As a test of their ability to write, each student had to pen a paragraph about themselves in a book entitled *Handwriting of Gardeners*. An early student was Joseph Paxton, who wrote: 'I was born in the year 1801 and at the age of 15 my attention was turned to Gardening and I was 2 years employed in the garden of Sir G O P Turner at Battlesden.'

Paxton went from the position of under-gardener at the Society's garden in Chiswick to head gardener at Chatsworth House in Derbyshire, home of the Dukes of Devonshire. He later designed the original Crystal Palace for the Great Exhibition of 1851 in central London's Hyde Park, then the park in

southeast London where it was relocated three years later. For his efforts he was knighted, the first gardener to achieve such an accolade.

After the RHS moved to Wisley, it set about establishing a school of horticulture and in 1907 opened a small laboratory as a study centre for student gardeners. Pupils studied for two years, at the end of which they had to pass exams, write an essay on an approved horticultural subject, and submit no less than 200 correctly dried and named plant specimens along with a collection of insects that were 'either injurious or helpful in Horticulture'. Successful students were awarded the Wisley Diploma. In 1952, the Society commissioned a hostel to provide accommodation for trainees. At the opening ceremony, the president, Sir David Bowes Lyon, said: 'I hope we may look forward to the steady emergence of a whole string of Joseph Paxtons.'

Over the past century, hundreds of students have undertaken horticultural training at the RHS gardens, and that tradition continues today. The Society now offers a range of qualifications including the one-year RHS Level 2 Certificate in Horticulture, RHS Level 3 Advanced Certificate in Horticulture and RHS Level 3 Diploma in Horticulture plus the three-year Master of Horticulture (RHS) Award. In addition, 14 students each year are admitted to the two-year Wisley Diploma in Practical Horticulture, which was revised and updated in the 1980s. Education has been a core aim in designing the new Bicentenary Glasshouse. It incorporates a Learning Space, Growing Lab and teaching garden, enabling visitors from schoolchildren to amateur gardeners and trainee horticulturists to gain hands-on experience of how glasshouse gardeners work.

ABOVE *Planting out winter bedding in Wisley's walled garden*

OPPOSITE *Trainees learn a range of horticultural techniques*

CHAPTER 6
plants on trial

If you climb the gentle slope of Battleston Hill at RHS Wisley, passing through Henry Moore's bonelike arch at the apex, you're rewarded with a view down on to the Portsmouth Trials Field. Here, parallel rectangular beds lie either side of a wide, grassy slope, their different-coloured crops imprinting the field with a kind of horticultural bar-code. Its summertime displays of delphiniums and dahlias are more regimented than the rambling rhododendrons on the east side of the hill, and more modest than the flamboyant springtime carpets of bulbs, but that's because they're fulfilling an important horticultural function.

The Kitemark of quality

In this field RHS experts put all manner of plants and vegetables through their paces to find out which ones are likely to perform best in our gardens. Those that pass with flying colours are given the Award of Garden Merit (AGM), the Kitemark of quality for garden plants. Each year, the Royal Horticultural Society updates the 7000-strong AGM list, enabling us to invest in plants that we know will resist attacks from pests, grow robustly and flower spectacularly.

'Some people in the trade are muddying the waters, because it's cheaper for them ... Our objective is that when gardeners buy a garden plant, they can be confident that it is correctly named.'

The idea of testing plants has been at the core of the RHS's work since its conception. Systematic plant trials began in the 1860s at the Society's Chiswick garden, and they continued there for some 40 years until increasing air pollution made the site unsuitable. Initially, the focus was on fruit and vegetables, but flowering plants such as cannas, asters and violas were also tested. When the Society was given Wisley in 1903, the trials continued at the new site. A decision was taken, after much debate, to give an AGM to cultivars deemed worthy garden plants by the Wisley Garden Committee. The first AGM was awarded to the Chinese witch-hazel *Hamamelis mollis* in 1922. As the trials continued, the Society issued a publication entitled *Some Good Garden Plants* to let gardeners know which varieties held the AGM-ranking. However, as the decades passed, some of these varieties disappeared from cultivation, while others were surpassed by better cultivars but remained listed. An overhaul of the system was clearly needed.

In 1993, the Society relaunched the trials scheme, rescinding previous AGM holders and providing a new list of 3600 approved varieties. The plan was to update this list every ten years. When the first review was announced in January 2002, it slashed 1000 plants from the list and added 889 new ones. Five years on, the Trials Field hosts anywhere between 40 and 60 separate trials at any one time, classified as either long-term or invited. Long-term trials are conducted on a continually rotating basis for the most popular ornamental groups, for which new cultivars are continually being bred. These include carnations, pinks,

ABOVE *High summer on the Trials Field at Wisley*

dahlias, chrysanthemums, iris and sweet peas. These are supplemented by 'invited' trials, chosen by the RHS. There are several reasons why a particular plant group might warrant such a trial. It might not have been tested for a while, or a flurry of breeding may have yielded new, unproven cultivars. Or sometimes there might be a muddle over plant names that a trial can help rectify.

Trial by committee

The RHS has 13 committees whose primary work is running the plant trials. Composed of plantsmen and -women, renowned growers, scientists, world-class experts on particular plant groups and leading garden writers, they provide advice on which trials to hold as well as conducting the all-important judging. Members of the four main floral committees – Herbaceous Plant, Rock Garden Plant, Tender Ornamental Plant and Woody Plant – who advise the Society and its members on their particular plant groups also assess the relevant trials. Then there is the Fruit and Vegetable Committee, plus a whole host of committees

dedicated to testing individual plant groups. Some of these have a long history: the Daffodil and Tulip Committee was founded in 1884 and the Dahlia Committee in 1912. Committee members include broadcaster and plant hunter Roy Lancaster, Great Dixter's head gardener Fergus Garrett and Lady Skelmersdale, who owns specialist small-bulb nursery Broadleigh Gardens, in Somerset.

Once the committees have advised the RHS on which plants to vet in a particular year, the Trials Office sends out letters and places an advertisement in the September edition of the RHS magazine *The Garden* inviting people to contribute seeds or plants. Plant trials consist predominantly of clonal cultivars, which can be reproduced only by vegetative propagation. Seed trials are conducted when comparing different open-pollinated or F1 hybrids, the latter being the first generation of seeds and plants from two distinctly different parents.

'Some people in the trade are muddying the waters, because it's cheaper for them to sow seed of, say, lavender 'Hidcote' [*Lavandula angustifolia* 'Hidcote'] and get 1000 plants than to propagate it vegetatively and get the true one,' explains Linda Jones, principal trials officer. 'So they put those plants out and say they are lavender 'Hidcote', but in fact they are variable because they have come from seed. You could call it lavender 'Hidcote from seed', but if you call it lavender 'Hidcote' you're cheating the public. That's the sort of muddle the trials sort out. Our objective is that when gardeners buy a garden plant, they can be confident that it is correctly named.'

In the glasshouses

Once the plants and seeds have arrived, Linda's team passes them into the care of the Propagation department, tucked away at the back of the old glasshouses at Wisley. Sam Gallivan, acting senior supervisor of the

ABOVE *Assessing the* Sempervivum *trial*

OPPOSITE *Preparing the beds during winter*

department, takes charge of the new arrivals. Sam began her career in horticulture at 16 and joined Wisley in 1996 as a gardener. A slow rise through the ranks followed from senior gardener and then supervisor to her current role. 'I've been in propagation right from the word go,' she says. 'I just enjoy the growing. You get to grow things from the tiniest of seeds to humungous 6-foot [1.8-m] plants, and it's still a mystery as to how and why it works. You know the science behind it, but you still can't quite believe that it can occur like that. The work's very varied. We do seed sowing, cutting, grafting – all sorts of propagation techniques. We get a chance to grow most plants at some point or another – we have a good bash at growing each one and try to learn something from it.'

ABOVE *In spring, the propagation house is full of seedlings destined for the Trials Field*

Sam carefully tends the plants sent to Wisley until they are ready to be transferred to the Trials Field, as well as planting seeds, pricking out seedlings and growing on these plants until they, too, are ready for the outside world. The conditions under which the plants are kept is carefully planned in advance, so Sam knows exactly how much water to provide and each feeding regime – even the pot size and spacing requirements. 'Once a year we all get together and discuss the best ways to treat the trial,' she explains. 'It's very much a joint decision between the different departments and the committee members. We follow a planner that is set out from the word go. For example, with this year's petunia trial, we planted the seeds in week 15 into trays, then pricked the plants out into modules, as suggested, and put the plants outside

to harden off in week 22. Because it is a trial you do have to keep to a specific schedule as best you can.'

Spring is a busy time for Sam as this is when she is propagating many of the seeds for the trials as well as tending to the trials plants. Her 'office' is essentially a group of three adjoining glasshouses connected by a corridor lined with a mixture of stray plants, filing cabinets, plus the tubes and dials of various climate-control systems. On a guided tour, she explains that the first of the glasshouses has a mist system as well as underbed heating controlled by a computer that enables her team to keep the temperature at around 8 °C (46 °F) and the humidity relatively high. One long bench holds an impressive array of cherry tomatoes, evenly spaced in matching black pots, while another has a few stragglers left over from the dahlia trial that has since been planted out on the Trials Field. 'The tomatoes were all sown on the same day and have received the same heat and watering, but you can see that some are more advanced than others,' says Sam. 'It really does depend on the cultivar. The red ones seem to grow well, while the yellow ones seem slower. We'll hold on to these until the first flowers have appeared.'

As well as managing the trials, Sam has to juggle other requests from various garden departments. These range from growing bedding plants for the Floral department to overwintering sub-tropical specimens such as bananas and, recently, propagating plants to populate the new Bicentenary Glasshouse. Most of the non-trial plants live in the third greenhouse and nearby polytunnel. As well as baby-sitting a permanent rhododendron collection, Sam is looking after several big pots of cannas, rows of strawberries destined for the Fruit department, a potted protea, in which a chaffinch has set up home, and

ABOVE *Sam Gallivan pricks out seedlings*

OPPOSITE *Gardeners prepare a bed for a new trial*

some rather sad-looking pots of South African nerines with yellow, wilted leaves. 'These guys have been living here because if they went outside the wet would kill them,' says Sam. 'They look droopy because they're going into their sleep time. They'll stay like that until late September or October and then throw up a flower spike. I'm hoping they'll get taken into the new glasshouse.'

Preparing and planting the beds

When Sam's main charges, the trial plants, are ready for transplanting, she hands them over to Jim England, trials superintendent, and Anna Stankiewicz, trials senior supervisor, in the Field Trials department. Just as Sam has the task of carefully managing the flow of plants on to her glasshouse benches and then outdoors for hardening off, so Anna has the task of working out what plants will go into which beds on the Trials Field. Most trials run for three years, but vegetable and seed ones are usually assessed after a single season.

'My role is to ensure that everything runs smoothly,' she explains. 'This is one of two sites at Wisley on which we conduct trials. The other is in Wisley village, plus there are also some trials conducted at Rosemoor and Harlow Carr. Arranging what goes where on the Portsmouth Field is the most difficult

aspect of planning. It's not good horticultural practice to keep growing the same plants in the same place, so things have to move around. For example, you can see we have sweet peas in this bed at the moment, but next year they will be somewhere else. We have to work at least two years in advance to make sure things are planned correctly. Size, space and crop rotation all have to be taken into account, so there's a lot of juggling.'

An important part of the job is making sure the bed is in the right condition to receive the plants. Much of the hard graft is mechanized, with beds prepared using tractor-driven Rotavators, but the trials staff also hand dig some of the beds. This is particularly the case if a crop has been on the field for a long time, because there is usually a build-up of weeds. 'When you hand dig you get much better coverage,' says Anna. 'You're physically turning each clod upside down – the top layer ends up at the bottom. If you use a machine it's quicker, but the machine mixes the soil much less effectively. You might rotavate a field, and two weeks later find the weeds have returned.'

Once the beds are prepared, the planting begins in earnest. On a late spring morning in 2007, it is the turn of the lettuces that Sam Gallivan has carefully raised from seed in the preceding weeks. Anna, Jim and others spend the morning rhythmically bending and planting three half-rows of Cos and semi-Cos cultivars, until the bare earth is slowly turned into a living green-and-red Damien Hirst dot painting. It is important that the planting of each individual trial is completed in a single day so the plants have an equal chance. With the lettuces, the job's done by early afternoon, but when there's a 100-m (330-foot) bed to fill the team is up against the clock. 'Gardening is perceived as a very relaxed profession, but in the Field Trials department we are closer to the commercial end of horticulture and often working to deadlines,'

ABOVE *Anna Stankiewicz cutting the mustard! It's used to condition the soil*

says Anna. 'You'll often find Jim and me running around completely stressed out because we have to achieve something by a certain time of day.'

As well as ensuring the trials plants get treated the same and planted on time, Anna is responsible for keeping them healthy. Land that has been continuously cultivated for as long as the Portsmouth Field tends to be prone to pests and diseases, so a certain amount of spraying is inevitable. However, staff try to limit the application of chemicals by using alternative products and processes where possible. One of the Portsmouth beds that is due to receive a planting of chrysanthemums has been sown with Caliente mustard, which will be rotted down and dug in to improve the soil structure and condition and suppress pathogens. 'Every year we have to sterilize the soil before planting chrysanthemums, as they are very prone to soil-borne pests

ABOVE *Gardeners plant out the chrysanthemum trial*

OVERLEAF *The Trials Field is a vibrant display of colour in summer*

and diseases,' says Anna. 'We used to use a chemical but recently decided to try the mustard. We have also been using predatory mites to control red spider mite on the dahlias. We try as much as possible to use products and methods that can be repeated at home by Joe Public.'

As summer approaches, the trials beds are at varying stages of growth. To the left of the path that divides the Portsmouth Field, the trial of small tulips is in the second of its three years, the once colourful springtime blooms now beheaded. These bulbs were planted in early 2005 and represent many of the tulips that grow wild in the mountains of Turkey, Crete, Iran and Uzbekistan. The cultivar names reflect these distant homelands: *Tulipa kurdica*, *T. montana*, *T. humilis* 'Persian Pearl' and *T. humilis* 'Eastern Spice'. In the neighbouring bed the ongoing trial of tall bearded irises is, by comparison, in full flowering glory. The blooms span the colour spectrum from cinnamon brown and sunset orange to pale blue through to lush black and purple. Their

ABOVE *The sweet-pea trial begins to bloom*

cultivar names are testament to their flamboyant nature rather than their provenance: 'Gypsy Romance', 'Black Sergeant', 'Cream Soda', 'Fiesta in Blue' and 'Crackling Caldera' are among the 110 entries.

Across the path, the trial of diminutive *Sempervivum* is no less spectacular. Here, dozens of spiky red cushions and neat green rosettes burst from a gravel-topped bed. In all, 302 cultivars are being tested between 2005 and 2008, ranging from the fast-growing *Sempervivum* 'Super Dome' to the quite delicately tinted S. 'Pink Puff'. The array proved so popular in its early days that the RHS opened up the beds so visitors could examine the plants at close quarters.

'We used to use a chemical but recently decided to try the mustard. We have also been using predatory mites to control red spider mite on the dahlias. We try ... to use products and methods that can be repeated at home by Joe Public.'

This is the time of year when keen gardeners flock to Portsmouth Field, hoping to see the delphiniums and other striking ornamentals in full flower. Beyond the *Sempervivum*, flashes of pink and purple among the green foliage of the sweet-pea trial suggest they will not have to wait long for the annual firework display to begin. 'We make an effort to make the trials presentable and accessible for the visitors,' says Jim England. 'With a lot of the trials we make two beds either side of a central path, and we put all the labels so the public can see everything.'

Judging for 'excellent garden value'

When the flowers or vegetables reach their zenith, it is time for the judging to take place. The assessors from the appropriate committee turn up on the field at ten o' clock sharp, equipped with a score sheet for the entries they need to scrutinize. They are on the look-out for plants that give 'excellent garden value'. The criteria for the Herbaceous, Woody and Tender plants normally include their vigour and impact, length of flowering period, susceptibility to disease and the stability of their form and colour. They must also be relatively easy to grow. The judges make several visits during the summer season to assess their development over time. At each visit the plants are judged individually and comments from the judges recorded by the Trials Office staff, both of how the plant is performing in the trial and how good (or bad) it is in the experience of the committee members.

Each genus of plant is also judged according to criteria that suit its individual characteristics. So daffodils have not only to look good but also the flowering stems must not flop over, and the flower heads must appear above the foliage. Sweet peas must have at least four flowers per stem, and vegetables have to taste, as well as look, good. With long-term trials where new cultivars of the same genus are being assessed, a scoring system is in place. Each plant is scored against set criteria; so the overall appearance is worth up to 35 per cent, the stem can garner 15 per cent, the flower can attract 30 per cent, and the general presentation of the flower is worth 20 per cent. The scores are analysed at the end of the trial, and the average tally forms part of the discussion as to which plants are worthy of an AGM.

ABOVE *Judges vote for their favoured cultivars*

Some comments made by judges on the score sheet of the 2007 *Abelia* trial provide an insight into what precisely they are looking for. The down-at-heel appearance of *A. schumannii* 'Saxon Gold' yields the following comment and no award: 'Has survived, some leaves bleached but not burned'. A more favourable result is achieved by *A.* x *grandiflora*; it is pencilled in as worthy of its AGM with the positive comment 'very attractive plant with a certain daintiness' and a unanimous six votes. 'There has to be a minimum of six judges for the assessment to take place,' says Jim. 'Also, a plant has to get at least six votes to be recommended for an AGM, and there has to be a ratio of three-to-one judges in favour. So if six people are for and two are against, the AGM will be awarded, but if six are for and three are against, it won't.'

Once the trial is over, the Trials Office staff produce a report, naming and describing the cultivars that have won awards. These are made available on the RHS's website. Some trials are also published as full-colour bulletins, including thumbnail photos, detailed descriptions and tables that potential purchasers can use to compare and contrast different cultivars. Before each report is published, the RHS botanists strive to identify and correctly name each entry. This is an important service for gardeners as it helps regulate the sometimes confused nomenclature of cultivated plants and encourages the use of the correct name in the horticultural trade. While naming plants may sound straightforward, as 'What's in a name?' on page 60 shows, that is often not the case. In a trial there may be large numbers of cultivars of uncertain attribution or origin. Or there may have been a proliferation of new names for cultivars that are suspected of being identical to existing ones. The botanists use floras, monographs, journal articles and nursery catalogues, plus the images and dried specimens held in the RHS Herbarium at Wisley, to help them in their work.

ABOVE *A plant must get at least six votes from the committee members to be awarded an AGM*

OVERLEAF *Jim England hoes the Cos-lettuce trial of 2007*

Inside the Herbarium

Specimens and photographs of plants in each trial are also added to the Herbarium to provide reference material of known species or cultivars. Wisley's present Herbarium dates back to the early 1900s when the RHS began accumulating specimens from the garden and wild plants gathered by the plant collectors it sponsored. Its collection expanded in 1936, when the Society acquired a large collection of European wild specimens from Frederick Hanbury, a cousin of Sir Thomas Hanbury who, in 1903, had donated the garden at Wisley. An earlier herbarium had been created when the Horticultural Society of London was founded but was unfortunately sold when the Society ran into financial difficulties in 1856. A century and a half on, the Herbarium concentrates on collecting reference material from garden

ABOVE *Preparing a new specimen for inclusion in the Herbarium*

plants because other herbaria, such as that at the Royal Botanic Gardens at Kew, focus on reference material from wild species.

'Kew has about 7 million specimens from all around the world, more than 90 per cent of which are wild collected plants,' explains RHS Herbarium Keeper Christopher Whitehouse. 'However, our Herbarium holds only 70,000 specimens, and its focus is almost entirely on cultivated plants, primarily ornamental ones. We very rarely have fruit or vegetable specimens – we're very much focused on garden plants.'

The trials provide a useful source of material on cultivars from individual genera. Although it is not always possible to preserve a sample of every entry in a particular trial, Christopher tries to obtain a sample to represent each taxon, a taxonomic group of any rank such as a species, variety or cultivar. The result is that the Herbarium is swelling by some 1000 specimens a year. They are housed in high-rise cream filing cabinets within the main room of the Herbarium, in Wisley's Laboratory building. On a guided tour, Christopher explains the process by which new plants are added. First of all each specimen is colour-coded using a chart a bit like a high-spec Dulux paint chart. Then it is pressed and dried, which involves placing a complete plant plus separate flowers or petals between sheets of acid-free blotting paper. This is weighted with bricks for 24 hours before being tweaked to make sure that the leaves and petals are quite clearly displayed. Several such specimens are then sandwiched between sheets of cardboard in a traditional press and placed in a trough-like drying cabinet. When the plants are dry, which can take anything from a week to a month, they are mounted on card with a covering of flimsy acid-free paper. Once

ABOVE *A dried specimen of* Helenium *'Ring of Fire' from the RHS's Herbarium at Wisley*

a *pro forma* is added, giving detailed descriptions of the flower, plant habitat, stem and leaves, the record is ready for filing.

The Herbarium specimens are used primarily to identify plants. RHS members who want to know the name of a particular plant growing in their garden can send a sample for analysis by the RHS botanists. As well as consulting Herbarium specimens, the experts can refer to the accompanying collection of botanical illustrations, black and white photos, colour transparencies and digital images to help identify the mystery plant. Where the Herbarium has really come into its own is in assisting National Plant Collection holders track down and identify rare or lost cultivars.

'We have a useful historic collection of paintings, made between 1920 and 1950, of award plants both in trials and at shows. These are of many cultivars that have now disappeared, so they are the only records.'

'They might be researching all the cultivars in their group, and they want to compare what they've been given under a particular name with what we've got under the same name,' says Christopher. 'We have a useful historic collection of paintings, made between 1920 and 1950, of award plants both in trials and at shows. These are of many cultivars that have now disappeared, so they are the only records. For example, we have a painting of the dahlia 'Tally-Ho' made in 1926 following a dahlia trial. In 1998, we had another trial of dahlias and someone submitted a dahlia 'Tally Ho', but it wasn't the same. Because we had the painting showing the original 'Tally Ho' was dark red, with multiple rings of petals, we were able to say conclusively that although his orange-red entry with a single ring of petals was called 'Tally Ho', it was not the original cultivar of that name.'

One of the most useful functions of the trials is to provide 'nomenclatural standards'. These are specimens of plants that have been acquired from the original breeder so there are no discrepancies over their identity. Dried records of these are held in green folders within the Herbarium, such as one labelled as *Helenium* 'Ring of Fire' that Christopher takes out of the Herbarium cabinet. 'This was raised, introduced and submitted to a trial by a Dutch breeder from Wijchen in the Netherlands,' he explains. 'If we carry out another trial of *Helenium* in 20 years time and a couple of nurseries enter 'Ring of Fire', and they're different, we know what it should be like because this one came directly from the raiser.'

Specimens preserved in this way can last for several hundred years. One specimen of lavender that Christopher produces is dated 1731 but still retains its characteristic form and mauve hue. This longevity is helpful, given that one in ten of the plants entered into trials throws up some confusion over its name. In the future, DNA testing of specimens may be able to provide incontrovertible evidence for the identity of cultivars, but at present the technology is not accurate enough to enable identification at this level. Until it does, the trials and the Herbarium specimens offer the best means to ensure that the plants you think you have in your garden are the real McCoy.

ABOVE *The original* Dahlia 'Tally Ho' *(left) alongside its namesake.*
As the former is believed extinct, the latter now carries the name

Testing times

Documents in one of the box files that line the walls of Principal Trials Officer Linda Jones's office highlight the role the RHS played in helping to secure reliable potato crops with which to feed the nation during the First World War. Within the Potato File 1916–36 are several letters together with a copy of the Food Production Leaflet no. 21, issued by the Board of Agriculture and Fisheries. The leaflet sets the scene by explaining that:

Wart Disease was first reported to the Board of Agriculture and Fisheries in 1901, but was certainly present in Lancashire, Cheshire, and other districts many years previous to that date. Of recent years the disease has become much more prevalent, and the cultivation of such varieties of potatoes as PRESIDENT, UP-TO-DATE, KING EDWARD and ARRAN CHIEF, all of which are highly susceptible to the disease, has increased the loss due to its ravages ...

But fortunately for the potato growing industry in many parts of the country certain

varieties of potatoes were found to be resistant or, rather, absolutely immune to the disease. This fact had been observed by growers whose land had become infected. They had noted that the disease was never found on such varieties as MAINCROP, ST MALO, KIDNEY, CONQUEST and others.

In 1916, at the height of the conflict, the RHS decided to conduct a trial into wart-resistant varieties of potato and invited several breeders to submit tubers for inclusion in the trial. A letter, dated 1 December 1916, from Fred J. Chittenden, director of the trials laboratory, to potato raiser and merchant William E. Sands of Hillsborough, Ireland, explains:

We are having a trial for cropping and cooking qualities immune from wart disease during the next year and would be glad if you would let us know whether you could supply 48 seed tubers of each of the following varieties and the lowest price at which you could supply them: Sir Douglas

Haig, King Albert, Leinster Wonder, Irish Queen and Shamrock.

In the reply to Mr Chittenden, Mr Sands agrees to send 48 tubers of 'Sir Douglas Haig', 'King Albert' and 'Leinster Wonder', and to do his best to send 'Irish Queen' and 'Shamrock'. He apologizes for his tardy reply, saying:

I must ask you to excuse me, but I have been extra busy as my last potato man left to join the colours last week.

The next document recording the chain of events is a Post Office telegraph to Chittenden from Sands with the simple statement:

Department of Agriculture Ireland refuse permission to export your seed.

In response, Chittenden writes to the Department of Agriculture in a letter dated 12 January 1917, explaining that:

We are particularly desirous of obtaining these tubers from Ireland especially as they are unobtainable from Scotland and as you know the difference in yield between English and Irish grown potatoes when planted in the South of England is extraordinary ... Our trials I think may be regarded as of national importance.

On 18 January 1917 comes the reply:

Referring to your letter of the 12th instant, I have to state that in the special circumstances the Department will be prepared to permit the export from Ireland of the seed potatoes which you require for experimental purposes.

And, on 29 March 1917, Mr Sands writes to Chittenden, confirming despatch of the tubers and requesting:

Please be careful when unpacking them as they are so long in the sawdust I would expect they would be sprouting. This has been most unfair to me for the trial the way the department has treated me which I hope will be taken into consideration ... I hope you will get them in good condition. I marked them very urgent.

On 5 April 1917 a letter was sent to Sands confirming that the tubers had finally arrived. And a typed sheet entitled 'Wisley trials 1917' confirms that all the wartime to-ing and fro-ing was worth it, at least for the Irish breeder: among the eight wart-resistant varieties listed as receiving the Award of Merit are 'Sir Douglas Haig' and 'King Albert' tubers supplied by William Sands.

ABOVE RIGHT *A poster advises gardeners on how to avoid potato blight*

OPPOSITE *Village life in wartime Britain: farm workers tend the potato field at Quantocks Farm, Somerset, about 1940*

RHS GARDEN TOUR **ROSEMOOR**
with Curator Christopher Bailes

"A horticultural sweetshop"

Enveloped by the wooded valley of the River Torridge in Devon, Rosemoor is the Royal Horticultural Society's most westerly garden. It was given to the RHS in 1988 by Lady Anne Berry, whose family had bought Rosemoor House in 1923 to use as a fishing lodge. After the Second World War, Lady Anne moved in permanently with her husband and young son. She described the garden she inherited as 'dull and labour intensive, typically Victorian with a great use of annuals around the beds'. But after meeting noted English plantsman Collingwood 'Cherry' Ingram while recuperating from measles in Spain, she became enthused about horticulture and spent the next 35 years filling her beds with 'rare and unusual things'.

When Lady Anne gifted the estate to the Society, it comprised Rosemoor House and a 3-ha (8-acre) garden, plus 13 ha (32 acres) of pasture. Since then, under the guidance of Curator Christopher Bailes, the Society has extended the estate to 53 ha (130 acres) by acquiring the surrounding woodland: 'We took over a private house with a characterful West Country garden containing a very eclectic mix of plants,' Christopher explains. 'We've subsequently added all the bells and whistles of an RHS garden, to show the range of plants and gardening practices possible in this part of the country. Although it is now a large, public demonstration garden, it has retained a tremendous character, derived partly from its setting but also from the use of local materials and techniques.'

The Society's first task was to develop a masterplan for the garden. The noted landscape architect Elizabeth Banks created a design that shifted the focal point away from Rosemoor House by building a new visitor centre and developing the neighbouring section of pasture into a series of formal gardens. Other parts of the farmland have subsequently been transformed into a bog garden and lake, a rock gully, and a fruit and vegetable garden. 'We have a lot of respect for the landscape,' says Christopher. 'Elizabeth Banks designed the new parts of the garden into the pre-existing field pattern, keeping the original field hedges. Because it's divided up into relatively small spaces, Rosemoor doesn't overwhelm you with its scale – rather it is quiet and intimate.'

If you enter the garden from the visitor centre, passing between two pairs of fiery, red-seeded maples (*Acer palmatum* 'Osakazuki'), you find yourself at the top of a flight of steps leading to a path defined by tall, meticulously trimmed yew hedges. This is bisected by the Long Border, a 150-m (500-foot) walkway bounded by beds of asters, anemones, euphorbias and rudbeckias, with the vista terminated at either end by an ancient, stately oak. You can turn off through the dividing yew, beech, box and holly hedges into one of six formal gardens: the Queen Mother's Rose Garden, the Shrub Rose Garden, the Square Garden, the Spiral Garden, the Foliage and Plantsman's Garden or the Potager, Herb and Cottage Garden.

OPPOSITE *Formal hedges and cultivated ornamental plants contrast with the woodland beyond*

Start at the southern end of the Long Border, and your first right turn will take you into the Queen Mother's Rose Garden. Here, octagonally arranged beds edged with neat box hedges display such gems as the pink-petalled ground hugger *Rosa* Baroque Floorshow 'Harbaroque' and the showy, white-flowered *R.* Swany 'Meiburenac'. Planting this and the neighbouring Shrub Rose Garden was something of a gamble for Christopher: the absence of any major rose gardens in the West Country and the fact that polluted city air is known to keep fungal diseases at bay had led people to believe that roses would not thrive in Devon's clean, damp air. But the test case proved to be a success. 'Today we're growing over 2000 roses from nearly 200 cultivars,' he says. 'If you took a poll of our visitors, roses would probably be the most popular plant.'

Across the way from the rose gardens are the Spiral and Square gardens, named for the geometric shape of the hedges that provide the backdrop to their herbaceous collections. As you circumnavigate the former, the colour flows in refined pastel hues from the silver leaves and pale yellow flowers of the American silverberry *Elaeagnus commutata* through the pink-blossomed *Cistus* 'Grayswood Pink' and purple bell-shaped flowers of *Polemonium* 'Lambrook Mauve' to the deep lavender shade of *Geranium* 'Johnson's Blue'. By contrast, the neighbouring Square Garden is bold and brassy, with its gold and purple foliage plus orange spires of

red-hot pokers, *Kniphofia* 'Atlanta'. This cultivar was grown in West Sussex but named only after being discovered in the grounds of the Atlanta Hotel in Tintagel, a short hop from Rosemoor on Cornwall's north coast.

At the northern end of the Long Border are the Foliage and Plantsman's Garden plus the Potager, Herb and Cottage Garden. The former has a modern feel, thanks to a recent overhaul by Christopher's team. One of the most striking borders contrasts spiky, striped phormiums and bronze hedgehogs of carex with smooth, golden-stemmed bamboos and the pure white bark of an elegant, overhanging eucalyptus (*Eucalyptus pauciflora* subsp. *niphophila*). Close by, espalier-trained whitebeams with huge, silver-backed leaves provide the walls for a stylish, rectangular seating area. 'We chose *Sorbus thibetica* 'John Mitchell' because it has the biggest leaves, but it's also the most vigorous,' says Christopher, ruefully. 'We've been struggling to keep it within bounds. But it's incredibly dramatic.'

After being bombarded with the textures, colours and scents of the formal gardens, it's almost a relief to pass through the oak gates at the northern end of the Long Border into the wide, natural expanse of the Stream Field. Here, designed planting has been abandoned in favour of nurturing wild-flower meadows, where grasses, buttercups and yellow rattle (*Rhinanthus minor*) thrive. The last named is a welcome sight to Christopher as this hemiparasitic plant helps weaken grasses, giving wild flowers more chance of becoming established. 'About ten years ago we started to leave our meadows uncut in spring,' he explains. 'Last year I saw the first *Dactylorhiza* orchids.'

Beyond the meadow, just past twin Tibetan cherries (*Prunus serrula*) with arresting metallic-red trunks, the path crosses a stream. If you take a left turn before the water, you'll embark on the lower woodland walk that meanders through an old plantation of Sitka spruce (*Picea sitchensis*). Turn right and you'll climb gently between the high-sided walls of the Rock Gully, where hardy golden-stemmed

ABOVE *Raised beds in the Potager, Herb and Cottage Garden*

OPPOSITE *Two thousand roses now thrive at Rosemoor*

bamboos (*Phyllostachys vivax* 'Aureocaulis') and delicate pink-blossomed rhododendrons rub shoulders with unfurling tree ferns among damp boulders of locally quarried sandstone. The Rock Gully was built to provide a tunnel beneath the A3124, which slices the garden in two. Beyond the underpass, water-loving gunneras spread out umbrella-size leaves at the top of a small waterfall that feeds down into the stream.

From the underpass, you can turn right and take the circular path around the new Bicentenary Arboretum, Christopher's latest project. His aim is to provide a living reference library of the world's trees around the circumference of a sloping 3 ha (7½ acre) meadow. Because saplings take a long

time to reach maturity, his team initially planted a range of fast-growing 'nursery trees' such as alders, poplars and willows. These defined the boundary of the meadow and provided shelter but are being removed as the arboretum's intended specimens start to flourish. When the arboretum is fully planted, a circumnavigation from the upper Bog Garden will take you through North America, Japan, China and the Himalayas and on to the Near East and northern Europe. If the world tour gets tiring, you can rest in the Palmer House Gazebo, an octagonal tower that stands on the upper edge of the meadow. Built in 1752 in the grounds of Palmer House, Great Torrington, it was moved to Rosemoor for reconstruction and renovation in the 1990s.

As you wander around the gardens' various compartments, you are likely to spot a wide array of hollies (*Ilex*) and dogwoods (*Cornus*). This is because Rosemoor holds the National Collections of these plants. As chapter 2 explains (see pages 58–9), National Collections are aimed at conserving Britain's plant heritage by maintaining as wide a selection as possible of species and cultivars in one location. The idea is to preserve varieties that might otherwise disappear from our gardens through changing fashions, disease or altered environmental conditions. Altogether, Rosemoor has 31 species and 47 cultivars of dogwood and 37 species and 120 cultivars of hardy holly. 'They form part of the gardens, and I like to think they are in the appropriate setting,' says Christopher. 'One of the hollies, *Ilex x altaclerensis* 'General Rougier', was found as a seedling here and is named after our first director Major-General Jeremy Rougier – although we noticed, after we named it, that the plant was female.'

The path from the new arboretum leads the way through an older planting of rare trees and on to the elegant, wisteria-hung Rosemoor House, where Lady

ABOVE *Cornus contraversa 'Variegata', part of the garden's National Collection of dogwoods, alongside the main lawn near Rosemoor House*

Anne first began creating a garden half a century ago. When she was planting, the climate was considerably different from today's warming world; Christopher has noted a discernible change in conditions even in his two decades as curator. As a result, plants that Lady Anne struggled to grow are now thriving around her old residence. 'In January this year the evergreen Chilean climber *Lapageria rosea* was still in flower,' says Christopher. 'Yet that's a plant we would not have even dreamt of being hardy here a few years back. And this Canary Islands holly used to be pinched back by frost each year, but now it's growing freely, and I have to keep lifting the crown of the tree above it to give it more room.'

Christopher is planning to redevelop the area immediately around Lady Anne's house to encourage visitors to explore the woodland on the hillside above. Once that is done and the Bicentenary Arboretum reaches maturity, Rosemoor will provide as wide a range of outdoor gardening experiences as any of the RHS's gardens. 'At Rosemoor you can take a country walk, or a garden walk, or you can be in the middle of an all-singing, all-dancing formal garden or in this classical, informal English woodland garden,' enthuses Christopher. 'It's endlessly varied. Being curator here is the most tremendous privilege, like being let loose in a horticultural sweetshop.'

ABOVE *Rosemoor House, where Lady Anne Berry began developing the garden half a century ago*

CHAPTER 7
flower power

Every year, as spring warms to summer, towns and villages around Britain begin looking that little bit brighter. Roadsides glow yellow with daffodils, pink geraniums sprout from public-park flower-beds and purple petunias cascade from the window-boxes of town-centre shops. The reason for this flurry of floral activity is the Britain in Bloom Campaign, organized annually by the Royal Horticultural Society. The largest contest of its kind in Europe, it encourages communities to make their locality cleaner and greener for the benefits of their inhabitants and visitors. All UK regions and nations operate independent campaigns, where judges visit communities within their area to assess which communities deserve to be nominated for regional and national awards. The best of the bunch go forward to the UK-wide assessment to find the overall Britain in Bloom winners.

Blooming nation

The roots of the contest date back to the 1960s, when Roy Hay, gardening writer and broadcaster and one-time assistant editor of the *Journal of the Royal Horticultural Society*, visited France on holiday. He found himself in the midst of the Fleurissement de France, a competition introduced in 1959 as a means of promoting civic pride and tourism. During his visit, the country was overflowing with flowers. 'Roy came back and said, "I can't believe it – every village is covered in colour. Why don't we do that in Britain?",' explains Jim Buttress, chairman of the judges of RHS Britain in Bloom. 'Roy started the British competition off in 1963 with the British Tourist Authority and the RHS. Towns and villages began taking it up, and it went on from there.' Initially involved only in a godfatherly capacity, by 2000 the RHS was to become entirely responsible for its organization.

Early rounds of the campaign had a reputation for rewarding large municipal-bedding schemes. Then, as councils began to encourage other forms of civic decoration, the hanging basket became an enduring symbol of the competition. Entrants soon realized Britain in Bloom's potential for helping to regenerate run-down areas and increase tourism. When the Devon village of Chagford won in 1972, the increase in traffic from visitors going to see the flowers led residents to demand they refrain from entering in future. Today, entrants are located in 18 regions and nations across Britain. There are 12 English areas plus Scotland,

OPPOSITE *Britain in Bloom: flower power in the streets of Minehead*

Wales, Northern Ireland, the Isle of Man, Jersey and Guernsey. Within these regions and nations, communities are assigned to ten population-banded categories. These include Large City (with a population of more than 200,001), Small Village (300 and under), Urban Community, Urban Regeneration and Coastal. Communities within each category are encouraged to compete with each other to plant and landscape trees, shrubs and flowers imaginatively, and find innovative ways to manage issues of litter, graffiti and vandalism. Each year

ABOVE *Floral displays like these at Abingdon on the Thames riverside have become an enduring symbol of Britain in Bloom*

every region or nation is able to nominate successful entries to represent it in the UK finals. The UK Britain in Bloom judges then award these finalist communities Gold, Silver, Silver-Gilt or Bronze medals (in 2006 there was a record number of Golds awarded, suggesting standards are on the rise). To ensure that effort is sustained over time, this round of assessments takes place in August the year after a community qualifies.

'There's a reason for that, and I'll tell you the story,' says Jim. 'Me and my mate were judging one day when a taxi driver pulled up and said, "Oi, are you one of those Britain in Bloom judges?" I said, "Yes, that's right," and he said, "Well, I tell you what, mate, none of those flowers was there last night." That's what we want to avoid.'

Jim started out as judge of the London in Bloom regional contest in 1975; then he became chairman of London in Bloom and eventually was asked to become involved in judging at the UK finals. Today, he's the chairman of the panel of 14 UK judges and in 2007 was allocated judging of the Coastal category. 'We're not there to nit-pick – we're there to get an overall picture and to see that there's a loved feeling about the place,' he says. Initially the judges visit unannounced. Then, when the formal judging takes place, the assessors meet the mayor and are given an itinerary. They then have between one and four hours, depending on the size of the community, to work their way through different sections, including floral displays in front gardens, pubs, restaurants, commercial premises and parks. There's a category for permanent planting of trees and shrubs, and there's also one on the Earth Summit's Agenda 21 and sustainability. This category is designed to assess recycling, water conservation, mulching and the amount of litter, graffiti and chewing gum. The fourth category is all about how members of the community have been involved in the campaign, such as places of worship, schoolchildren and local clubs. 'It's a lot broader than it used to be – it's about the whole community,' says Jim. 'Thirty years ago if you showed me 40,000 hanging baskets you were going to win. But now it's about the whole community keeping their town at its best for the whole year.'

> 'Thirty years ago if you showed me 40,000 hanging baskets you were going to win. But now it's about the whole community keeping their town at its best for the whole year.'

Seaside in bloom

The Regency seaside town of Sidmouth in Devon has been entering the Britain in Bloom competition for 35 years. Over this time it has won many floral competitions: it was the winner of Britain in Bloom Coastal Category in 2001 and 2005, and won a Silver award in the UK finals in 2003. Its success is thanks in no small way to the passion of resident Joy Seward, who has been involved from the start. Now aged 74, she is the president of the ten-strong Sidmouth in Bloom Committee that helps raise funds by hosting events such as coffee mornings and Berries and Bubbly afternoons, generates ideas for new horticultural displays, persuades local businesses to get involved by decorating their buildings and has even been known to print and distribute posters declaring, 'Watch out, the Britain in Bloom judges are coming soon.'

'The competition has taken over my life really. I don't drink and don't smoke – this is my hobby, and I'm very passionate about it. I think life without plants and flowers would be so dull.'

'The competition has taken over my life really,' Joy admits. 'I don't drink and don't smoke – this is my hobby, and I'm very passionate about it. I think life without plants and flowers would be so dull. As soon as they start growing in spring, I think, This is wonderful, it's a new year and a new beginning.'

Funding for Sidmouth's floral decorations come from a wide range of sources. Sidmouth Town Council and East Devon District Council provide major displays, such as the formal bedding in the town's parks. Then a number of commercial businesses and charity organizations chip in with other contributions. Around 40 enterprises helped fund the town's 2007 entry, including Sidmouth and District Hospitality Association, Sidmouth Stroke Club, the Blue Ball Inn, Sidmouth Garden Centre, Bedford Lawn Car Park and Oakdown Touring and Holiday Park. Waitrose is a big supporter: it paid for a new planter in the town centre, sponsored a public bench and installed a jungle-based display at its car-park entrance, complete with palms, grasses and a giant dinosaur fashioned from a box hedge. The Sidmouth in Bloom committee raises a further £10,000 each year to finance additional displays throughout the town. It then runs competitions to

OPPOSITE *A box dinosaur greets visitors to Waitrose in Sidmouth, one of the town's many floral displays*

SIDMOUTH

twin town
LE LOCLE

BRITAIN IN BLOOM
NATIONAL WINNER
FOR THE YEAR 2001

encourage all residents and local businesses to do their bit to keep the town looking its best all year round. Joy's personal contacts and powers of persuasion have worked wonders for the competition coffers in the past. 'One morning when we were short of some money, I phoned around some of my business acquaintances and managed to raise £2000 by lunchtime,' she explains, over a lunch of potted crab in her son's sea-front hotel.

A tour of Sidmouth in mid-June reveals the influence that Joy and her committee colleagues have had on the town. The perimeter flower-bed of the Triangle, an area of lawn close to the sea front, has been transformed into a sea-bed by the addition of several giant fish, a starfish and whelk, all made from plants. The creatures have been created by filling iron frames, made by a local foundryman, with carpet-bedding plants such as red and green sedum. 'We have to come and trim around the eyes with scissors sometimes, but apart from that they grow well and fill out their frames,' says Joy. The same technique has

been used at the fire station to create a living fire engine, complete with ladder. It decorates the front wall, beside a real ambulance. Blackmore Gardens hosts two more floral creatures. In one wide area of lawn stands a peacock, its head shaped using carpet bedding, its tail a flowing bed of pink, red and white busy Lizzies. With pointed beak and watchful eyes it towers over Joy. Not far away, in front of a stand of bamboo and cordylines, is a life-size donkey fashioned from wicker, with polished wooden hooves and geranium-filled panniers. 'Sidmouth has the largest donkey sanctuary in the world,' says Joy. 'They decided to sponsor this donkey to join in with the competition. We're going to hold a contest to name it, and raise even more money.'

In Connaught Gardens, a public park perched atop the red sandstone cliffs on the western side of the town, are various displays of cacti, succulents and sub-tropical plants. Care has to be taken when selecting what to plant here as parts of the garden bear the full brunt of the southwesterlies that blow in off the beach. The wreck of MSC *Napoli*, not far offshore, is a visible reminder of the strength of the storms that batter the southwest. In one of the more sheltered areas are flower-beds designed and planted by local schoolchildren. Shredded Wheat is the present major sponsor of the UK finals of Britain in Bloom, so five local schools each created a flower-bed with the theme of healthy eating. Considering some participants were only seven years old, the results are both

ABOVE *A starfish planted with carpet-bedding in the Triangle, Sidmouth*

OPPOSITE *Near by, a fish swims along the flower-beds*

colourful and innovative. Sidbury Church of England Primary School has created a smiley face, with banana mouth and strawberry eyes, from yellow and red flowers. A local college has re-created Shredded Wheat's logo of two hearts, while St John's School has produced a plate from plants and stuck a giant knife into it, alongside apples made from sage and bananas made from marigolds.

'This one's supposed to be a fruit salad with the different-coloured flowers representing plums, raspberries and so on,' says Joy. 'My brother designed the knife, my nephew cut it out, and my husband painted it,' she says. 'The schools were given a list of what plants they could have, how much they cost, how to plant them and the height they grow to. The children had great fun doing it. I do think if you can involve children when they're young they won't vandalize when they're older.'

Unfortunately one of two large pots costing nearly £400 each that the committee had purchased and planted was vandalized. Not to be beaten, the team immediately replaced it and, on a blustery summer's day, Joy goes to check it has been planted up to her specifications. 'I left a whole load of flowers to be planted in them but they've not been used,' she frets, calling the committee secretary on her mobile to find out what's happened and make sure the job gets done. From the churchyard, it's a short walk to Sidmouth's town-centre marketplace, so Joy goes to check how the floral decorations there are coming along. She is pleased to see that the new £600 tiered planters for

ABOVE *A flower-bed planted by local schoolchildren (left), and Joy Seward beside Sidmouth's famous peacock (right)*

OPPOSITE *Sidmouth's Hayman's butchers has won the 'small shop frontages' local competition many times*

which she helped raise money are bright with petunias and pansies. Sidmouth Parish Council helped fund these, along with Waitrose, the Chamber of Commerce and the Hospitality Association. Although the planters are costly additions to the town's floral displays, they contain water reservoirs so the flowers won't need watering very often. Many of the town centre's pastel-painted shops have added their own exhibits to the floral extravaganza. Hayman's butchers has several overflowing hanging baskets, along with pots of small conifers. Meanwhile, petunias and fuchsias tumble from the window-box of a nearby delicatessen. As Joy passes the shop of John Hollich, Hairdresser to Gentlemen, a man in a pink shirt rushes out, saying: 'Don't worry, Joy, I've got some more hanging baskets to come, yet.' This is despite the fact that his modest shop front already has 11 hanging displays. 'I just love it when all these flowers start appearing,' says Joy gleefully.

The competition is not only about flowers, though. In 2007, the RHS introduced a Bloomin' Wild theme to encourage communities to design and plant for wildlife. Rather than just installing neat rows of thirsty bedding plants and maintaining immaculately trimmed lawns, entrants are now encouraged to let grass grow long, leave dead trees for insects to inhabit and install bat and bird boxes to enable animals, as well as humans, to enjoy Britain in Bloom. Joy and the committee have taken this on board by developing an area of park on the outskirts of Sidmouth as a haven for wildlife. In a meadow known as the Knapp, two new benches made from recycled 'bags for life' and other plastic waste provide a place for people to relax. New interpretation boards illustrate creatures such as spined sticklebacks, pond snails and mayfly that dwell in and around the small circular pond. And instead of cutting the grass, Joy has instructed the council just to cut a swathe through it to allow people access to the pond and seats. The hope is that wild flowers will take root across the rest of the meadow and that insects will make their home in the log-pile lying to one side of the site. 'The competition's remit is wider than just growing flowers,' says Joy. 'We encourage recycling and persuade people to use biodegradable things. And for two years I've been involved with helping our country rangers and local schoolchildren to make bird boxes and bat boxes. We hope this will become a nice area for people to come and relax in.'

With Sidmouth aglow with floral arrangements, Joy can only wait for the day of judgement for the national round of the 2007 competition and hope for the best. That hasn't stopped her going and taking a quick peek at the competition, however. There are 11 other finalists in the Coastal category, including Great Yarmouth, which she recently visited to assess Sidmouth's chances against the opposition. She also went to look at nearby St Ives, which is competing in the Champion of Champions category, so is not a direct competitor this year. 'There's quite a lot of rivalry between us and St Ives, so we went and had a little look,' she admits. 'They're very good, but we have such wonderful parks – I think Sidmouth's got the edge, but then I would, wouldn't I?'

She's also set her sights further afield in her attempts to keep Sidmouth blooming for many years to come. In September, she's going to St Petersburg to celebrate her wedding anniversary and exchange ideas with the organizers of Russia in Bloom. This far-flung offshoot of the competition came about thanks to a Russian lady living in Sidmouth who approached Joy to see if she could

OPPOSITE ABOVE *Children find out what's living in the pond at the Knapp in Sidmouth*

OPPOSITE BELOW *Sidmouth's new Bloomin' Wild area has a pond, plus bird and bat boxes*

help set up a contest in her homeland. They persuaded Suttons Seeds to donate some seeds, and the competition took off. Recent participants include the communities of Gavrilov Posad, Chernogolovka, St Petersburg and Yaroslavl. 'I'm really looking forward to going,' says Joy. 'Apparently they even grow flowers in Siberia. Not so long ago the Russians were seen as our enemy, and I think it's wonderful that now we can go over there and see all these new floral displays.'

Community spirit

The idea of using flowers to build up community links and deter conflicts lies at the heart of a Britain in Bloom initiative introduced in 2004. The Neighbourhood Awards are part of the wider national campaign run by the RHS in collaboration with the regions and nations, and supported by the Department for Communities and Local Government's Cleaner, Safer, Greener Communities initiative. The Awards recognize the efforts of residents in small communities who are taking action to regenerate their local environment. While entries are not judged against each other, they are visited by Britain in Bloom experts who provide feedback and advice on how to develop current activities and encourage on-going improvements. Each entry is presented with an Award of Improvement, Merit or Outstanding Achievement. The Neighbourhood Awards section of the competition was introduced following a successful pilot scheme in Bradford. Shortly after Matthew Wilson had taken over as curator and head of site at Harlow Carr he was approached by Bradford Parks and Landscape Service, who wanted to see if it might be possible to create an awards scheme in which inner-city areas could compete. From five sites put forward, Matthew chose Ravenscliffe, a run-down residential area. Local residents had raised the money to build a new community centre and wanted to develop the surrounding area as a garden. 'The centre was in place, but the area around it was a bomb-site,' Matthew recalls.

ABOVE LEFT *Ravenscliffe's Gateway Community Centre, before its garden was developed*

OPPOSITE *Local people have helped plant the garden and brighten up the surrounds*

The smartly painted Gateway Community Centre stands amid a ring of pre-1920s semi-detached houses a ten-minute drive from the centre of Bradford. Only a few years ago, the estate's reputation for violence was so bad that bus and taxi drivers refused to go beyond the entrance, but today things are greatly improved. The community centre has helped to stimulate that change. With a café and classes such as yoga, rug-making and

'The centre was in place, but the area around it was a bomb-site.'

computer skills, it offers a place for locals to gather and socialize. The site was formerly occupied by Ravenscliffe First School, so the grounds around the building are substantial. The idea of the gardening scheme was to develop these into a recreational space that locals could create, maintain and enjoy. The organizers were able to get funding through various regeneration grants and so paid Bradford Community Environment Project to landscape an area at the front of the Community Centre. Once this had been done, Matthew took the entire Harlow Carr gardening team to the site, where they worked with local residents and schoolchildren to plant a range of trees and shrubs, many of which had been donated. Local people also transformed a derelict roundabout at the entrance of the estate into a community garden for residents to use as a place to relax and socialize. They received a Neighbourhood Awards Certificate of Merit for their efforts.

ABOVE *A team from Bradford Community Environment Project begins landscaping the area around the Gateway Centre*

'The centre and garden have made a lot of difference to people's lives,' says Gateway's receptionist and administrative officer, Janet McGill. 'Before, a lot of people got depressed that nothing was happening. They used to sit at home and do nothing, but now they come here. It's given people hope. It's made a great difference to me personally because before I came here I had not worked for 30 years.'

The garden stands to the right as you enter the Gateway Centre car-park. Two large boulders announce its entrance, and a path winds away from them around beds newly planted with heathers, lavender, broom, polyanthus, violas and a young *Magnolia* 'Heaven Scent'. 'We've tried to make it a touchy-feely garden,' explains volunteer Robert Sherry, a tall man with a greying ponytail, who lives near by and comes to the centre one day a week to help keep the garden tidy. Beyond the garden, towards the rear of the centre, Robert has

ABOVE *Local volunteers, including Robert Sherry (right), keep the garden tidy*

planted a series of apple, pear, plum and damson trees to create a mini orchard. The plan is to turn the remaining land into a wild-flower meadow. 'We tried planting wild flowers, but they didn't grow – it's all covered in dock leaves,' he says, ruefully. Meanwhile, at the front of the centre, to the left of the entrance gate, a new phase of work is beginning. On a large area of cleared earth, Matthew Wilson is planning to help residents create raised veg plots, and Robert is keen to start getting his hands dirty. 'My plot's going to be the biggest,' he says. 'I'm hoping to grow some veg for myself as well as supplying some to the Gateway. I already grow potatoes and carrots in my garden at home.'

Like Sidmouth, Ravenscliffe has experienced a few set-backs through vandalism, which have understandably dampened the enthusiasm of volunteers. Youths ripped off the roof of one of the structures in the children's playground, and they have sometimes pulled up plants in the garden. 'We just play them at their own game and plant them again,' says Robert, stoically. The trouble began when the garden was at an embryonic stage, and Matthew asked one of the contractors he uses at Harlow Carr if he would level the

ABOVE *Young gardeners keep the veg plots well watered*

OPPOSITE *With Gateway's small veg plots thriving, the plan is to build new, larger ones so locals can grow some of their own food*

earth for the garden. 'He got a call from the local police in the early hours to say that one of his machines was being chased through the streets of Bradford at five miles an hour with about 15 youths wedged all over it,' he says. Matthew is keen that the good work undertaken so far will continue, however. He is planning to take a group of interested locals to his own veg plot so they can see what can be achieved and to take a portable 3x3 m (10x10 foot) veg plot to Gateway to demonstrate veg-growing techniques.

'The way I see it is that if we inspire or involve only one or two people a year, that's one or two more people that are inspired and involved than otherwise would be,' he says. 'You make tiny, tiny incremental steps and along the way things happen like this upsurge in vandalism, and everyone's a bit depressed. But that's inevitable. The RHS doesn't have the resources to carry projects like this for ever, but we can go down there and inspire the local residents and lift them all up again. I genuinely believe that gardening is a great starting-point for connecting people with the natural world. It's proven that green spaces improve people's lives. It sounds naïve but once people make the connection with the wider environment they start to be better people.'

Far-flung friends

As well as forging national links through Britain in Bloom and its regional gardens, the Royal Horticultural Society has developed international links with many countries and communities abroad. Every year the RHS nominates two communities from Britain in Bloom to enter Entente Florale, the campaign's European equivalent. In its early years, the Society's membership spread geographically, until it spanned Europe, Poland, Russia, China, Singapore, the Azores, Libya, Egypt, Sierra Leone, Canada, the United States, Cuba, Brazil and St Helena. Members included directors of botanical gardens, head gardeners of private estates (including the Vatican gardens), naval doctors and dignitaries such as Sir Stamford Raffles, governor of Singapore, and US vice-president Liberty Hyde Bailey. Much of the work conducted by the Society abroad in the nineteenth century centred on British colonies. For example, former Secretary John Lindley advised the Admiralty on the planting of Ascension Island. The Society also had links with the Agri-Horticultural Society of India and Calcutta Botanic Garden.

During the First World War there were calls for enemy aliens to be expelled from the Society, to which it responded by saying that such aliens ceased to be members when they could no longer pay their subscriptions. After the Second World War, the RHS sent plants for the International Peace Gardens in Salt Lake City, Utah. In the intervening years, it has forged close links with the garden of La Mortola, the Italian home and resting-place of Sir Thomas Hanbury, who donated Wisley to the Society in 1903. The Italian garden became derelict after the Second World War, but in 1979 a restoration project began under the guidance of the University of Genoa. The RHS helped to arrange staff and paid for the cataloguing of the plant collection. It continues to play an advisory role. Today, the Society has partnerships with 20 gardens in France, two in Italy, one in Belgium and one in the USA, all offering free entry to Society members.

Not many people know that the RHS has a Japan branch, initiated after the Seibu Department Stores group sought advice on planting rhododendrons at a new park and botanical garden in Mount Agaki. The Society arranged for James Russell, renowned gardener at Castle Howard, to visit Mount Agaki and advise the company on its behalf. The idea of an RHS Japan branch grew out of the exchange, and the offshoot was formally inaugurated in 1986. Two years later, it launched its own journal using abridged translations of articles published in the Society's UK magazine, *The Garden*. Branch membership had reached 3000 by 2002. It has spawned four regional groups along with the Japan Hanging Basket Society, Japan Alpine Plants Study Group and the Container Garden Society. English gardening is now a popular pastime across the country. We, of course, have Japan to thank for introducing Zen-inspired garden design to the UK.

LEFT *A Japanese-style Zen garden*

OPPOSITE *La Mortola, the Italian home and resting place of Thomas Hanbury, who donated Wisley to the Society*

CHAPTER 8
grand plans

Visitors to Wisley during 2006 would have noticed an unusual amount of activity in a field in the far western corner of the gardens. Here, a previously undeveloped site had been allocated as the location for the Royal Horticultural Society's new glasshouse. After the first sod was cut in 2005, workmen moved in to clear the ground, dig out a new lake and slowly put together the imposing, curvilinear structure. The aim was to celebrate the Society's 200th anniversary of 2004 with a glasshouse that could demonstrate the full range of plants we can grow under glass, as well as having educational facilities to pass on knowledge gleaned over the decades. 'We identified the need for a new glasshouse back in 1994 when we were developing a masterplan for the gardens,' says Wisley's curator Jim Gardiner. 'We wanted to find a building that could be easily managed from a practical point of view but that would, at the same time, give us an iconic structure.'

ABOVE *An artist's impression of Wisley's new glasshouse before it was constructed*

The solution came in the form of a glasshouse from Dutch company Smiemans Projecten. The firm had developed a system for building unique glasshouses by putting together curving glass panels in different forms. In 2002, a research team from Wisley went to look at a few of their previous conservatories in the UK, Netherlands and Germany, and realized the system would suit their needs very well. Smiemans's architects worked with Jim to ascertain the building's footprint, height and general form, while landscape architects Colvin & Moggeridge, who had helped develop Wisley's masterplan, set about designing the interior. Jim was adamant he wanted the glasshouse to be very airy and open inside, without lots of individual compartments.

'One thing I didn't want was for people to be for ever opening doors and going from one glasshouse environment to the next,' he says. However, he did want to have Temperate and Tropical sections, so a minimum of two discrete environments would be required. The question was how to achieve the two demands. Smiemans architect Peter van der Torn Virjthoft came up with the idea of enveloping the Temperate part within the Tropical section.

'We identified the need for a new glasshouse ... when we were developing a masterplan for the gardens. We wanted to find a building that could be easily managed ... but that would, at the same time, give us an iconic structure.'

ABOVE *The glasshouse takes shape beside the newly dug lake*

A green icon for the twenty-first century

After two years of work, the glasshouse with basic environmental controls was in place by early 2007. But with only a few weeks to go until the official opening by the Queen and the Duke of Edinburgh, the internal planting and exterior landscaping were still at an embryonic stage. After plentiful rain initially, creating conditions akin to those of the Somme battlefields, the weather then dried up, leaving the earth hard, dry and dusty. Horticultural staff struggled in the heat to dig the beds and begin the exterior planting.

Inside, the basic layout and structure were in place, including a *faux* rock face designed by Colvin & Moggeridge to provide two levels. But only a handful of palms and cacti sprouted from the beds to hint at the future nature of the vegetation. As the day of opening approached it was a case of all hands on deck, until some 7500 internal and 80,000 external plants were bedded in and standing to attention. When the Queen arrived officially to open the glasshouse on 26 June 2007, she put one last tree in place, a *Cornus kousa* 'Wisley Queen', to commemorate the auspicious occasion.

OVERLEAF *Water spills over a ledge in the new glasshouse*

ABOVE *Entertainers at the opening ceremony*

OPPOSITE *Wisley staff pack up plants for transporting to the new glasshouse*

Now open every day to the public, the glasshouse is a grand addition to the Society's horticultural and educational attractions. The structure covers twice the area of Wisley's previous greenhouses. As large as ten tennis courts and as high as three double-decker buses, its shape brings to mind the curves of a Mogul palace. Panes of 3.5x2 m (11½x6½ foot) toughened glass, bent into place when fitted, let in the maximum amount of light. The internal structure is arranged so that the Tropical section lies on the south side to capture as much warmth from the sun as possible, with the Temperate zone on the north side. A sophisticated computerized system controls the internal environments according to settings programmed by the horticultural staff. Heat coils are on hand to provide extra warmth if the sun's power is not enough, while fans continually direct heat down from the ceiling. Should the conditions get too hot, light-activated blinds provide shade to prevent plants from scorching. These also close at dusk, keeping in 60 per cent of the glasshouse's warmth at night. In the event of overheating, vents in the roof open up but close automatically if the wind builds to potentially damaging speeds.

Because many of the green inhabitants thrive in moist air, water is projected through tiny nozzles at high pressure to create a fine mist whenever the humidity drops below a set threshold. In the Tropical section, this is 65–70 per cent, while in the Temperate section it is slightly lower at 60 per cent. Rain-water gathered on the roof is filtered using ultraviolet light and then adjusted slightly to increase its acidity before it is used for watering. Any excess travels down pipes in the centre of the solid structural pillars that anchor the glasshouse to the ground. This is then released into the horseshoe-shape lake lying to the south. Although there are only the two main internal sections, Temperate and Tropical, the computerized environmental-control system enables horticultural staff to produce slightly different conditions within these large, open areas. This has allowed them to arrange the plants in three sections: Moist Temperate, Dry Temperate and Tropical. The state-of-the-art structure now takes its place alongside the Eden Project biomes and Kew's Davies Alpine House as a classic glasshouse for the twenty-first century.

Inside the zones

As you pass through the arched front door, you enter the Moist Temperate zone. Ahead lies a jungle, in which glossy-leaved *Rhododendron* 'Jabberwocky' and crimson begonias flower beneath unfurling tree ferns in a bed backed by the rocky cliff. Fashioned from glass-reinforced concrete placed over a steel frame, the cliff was moulded from real quarry faces in Devon to give a natural look. Water spills over its upper ledge, dropping 5 m (16 feet) to a water-lily pond below. Planted around the margins are tall fans of bird-of-paradise (*Strelitzia reginae*) leaves and fast-growing red-leaved banana plants (*Ensete ventricosum* 'Maurelii'). To one side, the branches of a large brugmansia (*Brugmansia* x candida 'Grand Marnier') bend under the weight of 30-cm (1-foot) long tangerine trumpet-shape blooms. Beside these permanent plantings, a section has been deliberately set aside for more ephemeral floral exhibitions. For the opening ceremony, the space was filled with huge bronze urns topped with slender stems of lilies; among them were showy pink *Lilium* 'Sorbonne' and white and yellow *L.* 'Time Out'. 'In November we'll have our own firework display here of Charm and Cascade chrysanthemums,' says Jim. 'This big open space provides the opportunity to do it. It will be a horticultural theatre.'

OPPOSITE *A path leads visitors around colourful tropical and temperate plantings in the new glasshouse*

Beyond the splendid roaring waterfall, the path gradually rises and the moist temperate plantings give way to a drier flora. Here, in a gravel-topped bed, are cacti such as tall, spiny organ-pipe *Lemaireocereus* and tight, prickly balls of *Echinopsis bruchii*. In pride of place is a dragon tree (*Dracaena draco*), which hails from the Canary Islands. It has thin, dark strips for leaves that spill over a palmlike trunk. In nature, dragon trees live to a ripe old age. One growing in Tenerife is believed to be 650 years old, while a specimen that blew into the sea in 1868 was calculated to be 6000 years old. This zone is designed to show the range of plants that grow in the deserts of the world. Many of them have adaptations that help them survive the hot, dry conditions: some have fleshy leaves that store water, others have spines instead of leaves to reduce evaporation, and many have silver leaves that help to reflect the sunlight. The plants grow in the wild everywhere from Mexico to South Africa. 'We're not a botanical garden constrained by having to make a geographically arranged display,' says Jim. 'We're very much about gardening under glass and showing just what can be achieved.'

'We're not ... constrained by ... a geographically arranged display. We're very much about gardening under glass and showing just what can be achieved.'

Leaving the arid collection behind, the path continues past a bench of carnivorous plants through a sliding door into the Tropical zone. Here, if you continue straight ahead, you encounter a pond, vegetated with water-lilies and a large clump of elephant's ear (*Colocasia esculenta*). So named because of its giant leaves, this plant produces taro, a staple food for many who live in Southeast Asia. Other plantings at ground level are highly colourful, including vibrant crimson and yellow cones of *Guzmania* 'Graaf van Hoorn'. If you take a left turn just as you enter the Tropical zone, you walk uphill to the top of the rocky outcrop. Now you are level with the crowns of palms and can look down on dappled maroon and white phalaenopsis orchids and the red spiky flowers of *Guzmania* 'Mohican'. Staying at the top, you pass back through into the Temperate zone, then wind down to ground level again. Now, the darkened cavern of the Root zone lures you to investigate the subterranean world.

Jim's aim in creating the Root zone was to help educate people as to the importance of this hidden part of the plants. 'I came up with the idea when I

visited New York Zoo,' he says. 'A section in the gorilla enclosure was dedicated to explaining what goes on beneath the forest in the Congo, the gorillas' natural home. I wanted to emulate that here.' The Root zone is designed to make you feel you have travelled beneath the soil. On entering, you learn that people in 21 countries rely on roots and tubers as their main source of food and that a hormone produced in roots tells shoots to grow more slowly when water is scarce. In the centre, giant 'roots' dangling from the ceiling hold TV screens showing time-lapse footage of plants emerging from rippling earth and the effects of rain deluges on seeds. Around the perimeter, porthole windows reveal common products made from roots. There are jars of horseradish sauce (from *Armoracia rusticana*), potato crisps and ginger as well as cancer drugs made from the Himalayan May Apple (*Podophyllum hexandrum*). At the exit is a quote from Leonardo da Vinci that reads, 'We know more about the movement of celestial bodies than about the soil underfoot.' The hope is that by the time you leave the Root zone you will have learnt a little more.

ABOVE *The curves of the glasshouse are reflected in the adjacent lake*

Coming attractions

The landscaping around the glasshouse was designed by Tom Stuart-Smith. Now a highly respected plantsman and landscape designer in his own right, he began his career as the assistant to Elizabeth Banks when she designed the RHS's garden at Rosemoor in the 1980s. A formal arrangement of rectangular beds lies close to the glasshouse entrance, some planted with coloured geraniums, hellebores, grasses and rodgersias, others with beech cylinders. With distance, the beds then sweep away from the structure in a series of crescents mirroring the curve of the lake. These connect the new landscaped area to the established neighbouring parts of the garden such as the Fruit Mount and Alpine Meadow. It will be five years before the full garden structure becomes apparent. Meanwhile, the old glasshouse site presents the opportunity for new developments.

'It's right in the centre of the garden, and temporarily we will use it for changing displays so that we always have something different to bring people back to,' says Jill Cherry, director of Gardens and Estates. 'We're thinking of having a really large sunflower or corn maze there for the next year or two.'

All four of the RHS gardens have grown incrementally over the years, so Jill is presently helping to develop new masterplans for each of them. These plans will ensure that the unique features of each garden are developed while still retaining an RHS identity. The plans will be in place by the end of 2007. 'Each garden has a regional identity and a unique character, according to its history or the way it sits in the landscape,' says Jill. 'We want to make the most of the opportunities each of the gardens has to offer. We might do that by holding events to celebrate what's special about a particular garden, by having a festival when, say, the magnolias are in flower. Or we might use the garden as a venue for an event such as a concert. Rosemoor is very interested in hosting cultural activities, and it already has some collaborations with the Two Moors Festival. I could see that over time they could really develop those.'

Rosemoor's history also provides some potential for development. Close to the spruce woods at the bottom boundary of the garden is an abandoned leat, or canal, that was once used to carry lime from the port of Bideford to lime kilns on the site. The lime was burnt and then spread on the surrounding fields to increase fertility. The hope is to restore the canal basin and to open a public walkway from Rosemoor's woodland car-park along the line of the leat to the basin, and allow visitors to see the lime kilns. 'We'd really like to make more of that as a historical feature and garden feature, to tie Rosemoor back to its roots,' says Jill.

Hyde Hall is planning to draw on its history, too. Presently only 10 ha (25 acres) of the 145-ha (360-acre) site is developed; the rest is fields. A map from 1716 shows the farmhouse at Hyde Hall set amid a network of fields and, when you stand in the gardens, you can trace some of the old boundaries via the mature oaks planted along them. 'We want to take those as our starting point and reconnect Hyde Hall with that landscape,' says Jill. 'We shall be building a new car-park, visitor centre and shop to accommodate many more people than the 100,000 visitors we currently attract. We want the garden to become a gateway to the historical Essex countryside.'

In the north of the country, Jill hopes to make more of the natural landscape at Harlow Carr by creating a new lake and highlighting the natural watercourse

OPPOSITE *Beech cylinders form part of the exterior planting around the glasshouse*

that runs through the garden. The lake will help to prevent flooding and provide a means to store water. 'We want to make the garden read back and forth across the stream,' she says. Curator and Head of Site Matthew Wilson is keen to develop Harlow Carr in a sustainable way that works with nature as much as possible. He has plans to build on the garden's environmental credentials by constructing a 'deep green' eco-building to house a library and learning centre. The outside will be landscaped along a theme of 'you are what you eat' to educate visiting schoolchildren as to where their food comes from.

'Although my family were not by any means wealthy, growing up on a nursery meant I had a very privileged upbringing in terms of the space I had and being able to connect with the countryside,' says Matthew. 'Once you've made the connection with plants you can then take that much further, which is what I'm interested in doing.'

Back in the glasshouse at Wisley, the Society has similar ambitions to engage new audiences in gardening. As well as a Learning Space and Growing Lab, the centre has an education garden complete with an environmentally designed shed, raised beds planted with lettuce, potatoes and herbs, as well as compost heaps to demonstrate the importance of recycling organic material. The hope is that as new people become involved in gardening, they will begin to understand why plants are so important to our everyday life and why we need, more than ever, to protect the natural world we inhabit.

'Traditionally our members and visitors have tended to be in the older age bracket ... However, we feel we have a strong role to play in opening younger eyes to gardening and the environment.'

'Traditionally our members and visitors have tended to be in the older age bracket, because many people don't come to gardening until they're older,' says Jill Cherry. 'However, we feel we have a strong role to play in opening younger eyes to gardening and the environment. When I grew up I used to go round gardens with my dad. I took from that an awareness of the value and beauty of plants and the natural world. Now I want us to make that connection with the younger generation. Our challenge for the future will be to create enough adventure and stimulation for a younger age group, while still retaining the tranquillity that is so enjoyed by our older visitors.'

OPPOSITE ABOVE *One trend for the future is for less formal, more naturalistic planting*

OPPOSITE BELOW *The Society aims to combine traditional garden elements with innovative new features*

Growing with glass

People experimented with the creation of artificial climates for growing plants as far back as Roman times. Then, farmers protected their crops by placing them beneath sheets of mica, a type of mineral that splits easily into layers. An early glasshouse was found in the ruins of Pompeii, which was destroyed by an eruption of Mount Vesuvius in AD 79. During the Middle Ages, as citrus plants became fashionable, wealthy landowners built temporary screens around their precious fruit trees. Slowly, more permanent buildings, known as orangeries, replaced them. These had large windows but a solid roof.

The Royal Horticultural Society's long tradition of growing plants under glass began when it acquired its garden at Chiswick in 1821. In those days, wood and masonry were the primary materials available for building conservatories. Heated by braziers or hot air piped through flues from external boilers, these created conditions that were hot, dry and relatively dark compared to those of later glasshouses. An alternative method for growing fruit at that time was simply to dig a pit in the ground and cover it with glass. Within a decade, the garden boasted 140 m (450 feet) of glazed pits and 120 m (400 feet) of hothouses.

Glasshouse technology soon evolved, however. Not long after Sir George Mackenzie had read a paper to the Society extolling the virtues of the dome as a potential design for glasshouses, John Claudius Loudon invented a wrought-iron glazing bar that

could be made in curved sections. This made possible the curvilinear constructions that would let in a great deal more light than standard designs. In 1840, a few years before the Great Stove at Chatsworth and Kew's Palm House were created, the Society commissioned for its garden at Chiswick a wrought-iron curvilinear conservatory. It was described as the 'first example of a solidly engineered cast-iron barrel vault over a hall' and was soon housing the Society's collection of camellias and Australian plants.

Over the years, this great glasshouse was supplemented by other conservatories. These included an orchid house, a conservatory built by James Hartley of Sunderland and used to house exotic conifers sent back by RHS plant collector Carl Theodore Hartweg, a rose house that proved unsuitable for growing roses and additional orchard houses for growing fruit. Two more conservatories were built in the 1850s by Henry Ormson and James Gray. By now, heating methods had changed to steam and hot-water heating, providing warm, humid conditions that were suitable for rearing many of the sub-tropical plants brought back by Victorian plant hunters.

When the Society moved to Wisley in 1903, the garden had no glasshouses. So, in 1904, plans were drawn up for a range of conservatories that were completed the following year. These were located in front of the Laboratory, where the canal now lies. They initially housed grape-vines and figs moved from Chiswick, plus peaches and melons. After the Second World War, major repairs were needed, and the Society commissioned a range of glasshouses to be built close to what is now known as Weather Hill. Extended at various times in the intervening years,

these served the Society until the new Bicentenary Glasshouse opened in 2007.

If you go into the new glasshouse today and climb the path that leads above the waterfall, you'll encounter two staghorn ferns (*Platycerium bifurcatum*), high up on a ledge. Dark green, with bifurcating leaves that give them a seaweed-like appearance, they were initially brought to Wisley from Chiswick to inhabit the new glasshouses built a hundred years ago. Now, safely ensconced in another new glasshouse, they stand as a symbol of the Society's distinguished history of growing plants under glass and its ongoing search for horticultural excellence in all fields of gardening.

OPPOSITE *The glasshouse will demonstrate the range of plants that can be grown under glass*

RIGHT *Hidden away at the top of the waterfall are two century-old ferns that came from the RHS's Chiswick garden*

RHS GARDEN TOUR HYDE HALL
with Curator Ian Le Gros

"An opportunity to inspire"

The Royal Horticultural Society's estate at Hyde Hall dates back to the late fifteenth and early sixteenth century when it began life as a working farm. When Dr Dick and Mrs Helen Robinson acquired the estate in 1955, the farmhouse garden comprised a lawn of half-metre (2-foot) high grass, a central rose bed, pampas grass and eight trees. Although not experienced gardeners, they slowly tamed the wilderness around the farmhouse, planting trees, rhododendrons, a herbaceous border and a vegetable garden. The Robinsons set up the Hyde Hall Trust in 1976 and donated the garden to the RHS in 1993. It's been opening to the public all year round since 2002, 'a 25-acre [10-ha] garden sitting on top of a windswept hilltop in Essex, with about 360 acres [146 ha] of radiating farmland around it, which the Society owns,' explains Curator Ian Le Gros.

The environmental conditions at Hyde Hall set it apart from the other RHS gardens. It has a topsoil of heavy loam at best, which rests on an under-layer of clay. As well as being exposed to the wind, the garden receives just less than 600 mm (24 inches) of rain a year, not far off the lowest rainfall in the UK, indeed two-thirds of the national average. 'We bake in the summer, but because of the clay when it rains everything gets very soggy very quickly,' says Ian. 'So it's not an ideal place to have a garden at all. However, it gives us notoriety and the opportunity to inspire and educate people

as to how you can garden in Essex with great results. But we do have to go to great efforts to get it garden-able – we put more money into the soil than we do on top of it.'

Enter the Hilltop Garden in summer, passing beneath an oak pergola hung with heavy blooms of wisteria, and it's clear the Society's efforts have not been in vain. Straight ahead is the koi-filled Upper Pond, topped with water-lilies and bounded by a deep fringe of green, containing irises and hostas. To the right is a large lawn that slopes south. A herbaceous border with sunshine-bright *Kniphofia rooperi*, purple-leaved *Heuchera* 'Silver Scrolls' and pale spires of *Lupinus* 'Ivory Chiffon' stretches along its western flank, while packed rose beds provide a central feature. If you sit on the stone seat at the southern end and look up towards the farmhouse, you see the roses and entwined clematis grade from pinks and mauves through sunset yellows and back to pink again. 'We're good at growing and pruning roses up here,' says Ian.

More roses, growing along a 30-m (100-foot) rope walkway, lead you along the southern edge of the formal garden to the Lower Pond. Here, thick-stemmed gunneras stretch for the skies, while elegant *Salix babylonica* dangle their branches just above the water. A gravel path leads to the Shrub Rose Garden, a scented jungle, where tall white-flowering spires of *Molinia caerulea* rub shoulders with round-headed purple alliums and pink foxgloves, and the sunset hues

OPPOSITE *Hyde Hall's Upper Pond, formed from the original farm pond, is topped with water-lilies and is a haven for waterside plants*

of *Rosa* 'Aurora' contrast with the purple blooms of *R.* 'Nuits de Young'. Immature plants and climbers are helped by canes and frames fashioned from hornbeam twigs, pruned from the garden. 'We always think of how we can use material generated by the garden,' says Ian. 'Recycling is a vital part of gardening.'

Beyond the Shrub Rose Garden, you enter the Woodland Garden, a collection of rhododendrons, magnolias, camellias and other acid-loving plants initiated by the Robinsons. This leads to a new area of the garden that Ian and his team have totally redeveloped and renamed the Robinson Garden, after its former owners. A curved wall, built using 260 tonnes of granite and 93 tonnes of paddle stones, encloses two large dells, in which some 150 species of rare and unusual perennials, including tree ferns and hostas, are beginning to thrive. 'The wall was put in only two weeks ago, and we've

already got wrens nesting in it,' says Ian proudly. This part of Hyde Hall was formerly called Hermione's Garden, after the statue that stood in it; now one of the two new English oak bridges that cross the area has been named Hermione's Bridge to continue the tradition.

Ian is keen that Hyde Hall remains in touch with its roots. The tithe map of 1716, drawn by Benjamin Fallowes of Maldon, shows the farmhouse in the centre of 20 or so fields. Many of the original field boundaries remain; Ian has begun re-introducing names that appeared on the map. Areas of the estate such as Clover Hill and Road Field are named according to the 1716 plan. 'The map was drawn in pre-Ordnance Survey days,' explains Ian. 'Having been trained as a land surveyor, I can appreciate what the cartographer was trying to convey in that drawing.' Ian is also keen to make use of the

ABOVE *Hyde Hall looks out across the Essex countryside*

surrounding landscape, for instance by deliberately framing a distant church spire with plants or by stretching the formal garden's boundaries to incorporate mature trees in the surrounding fields. 'We've learnt that we can borrow views – for example there's a church at Woodham Ferrers that we can make use of. And by spreading the garden into the tree belt, the garden will become part of the countryside and the countryside will become part of the garden,' he says.

One of the last areas of farmland to be brought under cultivation by the Robinsons was the Old Pig Park. Until 1968, it housed sows that had helped them clear the land when they began work on the garden. Once the pigs had gone, they planted shrubs and trees such as crab apples (*Malus* species). The Society renamed the garden in honour of the Queen Mother after her death in 2002. Today, Ian is slowly redeveloping this section of the garden. So far he has replaced a conifer windbreak with a hornbeam hedge, planted up snakeshead fritillaries and crocus on the bank that edges the garden and introduced new *Malus* trees such as 'Winter Gold' and 'Mary Charlton' to replace older ones affected by fireblight (*Erwinia amylovora*).

'The Queen Mother's Garden was always a poor relation of the Hilltop Garden, but it has a wonderful atmosphere,' he says. 'Redeveloping an area like this is a ten-year project – there's no way you can do it overnight, especially if you want to keep the old characteristics. The Hilltop Garden is very much about shoe-horn planting, but here we are leaving things more open. In five years' time they will have grown together and will look nice.'

Beyond the Queen Mother's Garden is the North Meadow, a 0.8-ha (2-acre) field that was formerly farmed. The previous curator had sown it with wild flowers, this being a more sustainable way to manage the surrounding landscape. It is a policy that Ian is perpetuating, and the meadow now hosts more than 50 species of wild flower. The reservoir in the North Meadow, fed by storm drains, enables the garden to be self-sufficient in terms of its irrigation. The water is recycled by simply being pumped back up the hill for use in the garden. This is important, given that Essex imports 75 per cent of its water from other counties. The hay is cut and baled in July and August. In the distance, on the estate's northern boundary, a forest of young tree saplings is slowly but surely beginning to take root. Over time, this will become the Wild Wood, with some 55,000 trees, covering 30 ha (74 acres).

By limiting fertilizer and pesticide use at Hyde Hall, Ian and his predecessors have encouraged plentiful insects to take up residence in the garden. An interesting visitor has been the brown hare, which has taken to eating the tender young plants

RIGHT *Hyde Hall's Plant Centre and Shop is a good source of its emblematic drought-tolerant plants*

that Ian's team have introduced to the Australia and New Zealand Garden. For this reason, a sturdy metal fence separates this section of the garden from the other parts. Inside is a wide range of southern-hemisphere plants including spiky bronze clumps of *Carex comans*, bushes of *Callistemon citrinus* with crimson bottle-brush flowers and even moisture-loving tree ferns. Despite coming from the other side of the world, most are thriving. 'It's probably a bit too dry for the tree ferns, but the other plants grow well,' says Ian. 'Everything planted here is available to gardeners through the *RHS Plant Finder*, and 70 per cent of them are hardy.'

The Australia and New Zealand Garden is a natural neighbour to the Dry Garden, for which Hyde Hall has become famous. Officially opened in 2001 it contains some 5500 plants representing more than 850 different species and cultivars from every continent apart from Antarctica. All the plants originate from arid climates, such as southern and central Europe, southern Africa, California, South America, Australasia and central Asia. The result is an eclectic mix of colours and textures. White thistle-like stalks of *Eryngium giganteum* overshadow pin-cushion clumps of *Santolina virens* 'Primrose Gem', while feathery green fountains of *Stipa tenuissima* grasses curve at the whim of the wind. Many of the plants exhibit adaptations that help them survive in harsh, dry regimes, such as the silver leaves of *Cyanara cardunculus* that help reflect the sunlight and the thick, leathery leaves of *Sedum* 'Herbstfreude' that are able to retain water.

'The Dry Garden is an amazingly effective garden, with no rainfall and no fertilizer applications,' says Ian. 'It's an example of what can be achieved if you understand the soil, the climate and the types of plants that will succeed under those conditions.'

Garden of the future? The Dry Garden shows what can be achieved without watering

INDEX

ACKNOWLEDGEMENTS

The author would like to thank everyone who gave up their time to help provide material for this book. These include: RHS staff at Wisley, Harlow Carr, Hyde Hall, Rosemoor and Vincent Square; Simon Pugh-Jones and pupils at Writhlington Business and Enterprise Specialist School, Radstock; staff and pupils at Pinewood Infant School, Farnborough; staff and pupils at St Bartholomew's C of E Primary School, Armley, Leeds; staff and volunteers at the Gateway Centre, Ravenscliffe, Bradford; Elizabeth Cartwright-Hignett, owner of Iford Manor; Joy Seward, President of the Sidmouth in Bloom Committee; Chelsea exhibitors Suzanne Gaywood, Anthea Guthrie and Alan Gardner; Michael Ibbotson, a director of Colvin and Moggridge.

PICTURE CREDITS

BBC Books would like to thank the following for providing photographs and for permission to reproduce copyright material. While every effort has been made to trace and acknowledge copyright holders, we would like to apologize should there have been any errors or omissions.

Alamy: Tibor Bognar 194; Keith Glover 95; RHPL 177; SC Photos 43; TNT Magazine 195
BBC: 76, 82, 84, 127, 200; Cameron Shaw 72, 123, 124, 130
Bridgeman Art Library: Private Collection/© Taylor Gallery, London, UK 50–51
Corbis: Ray Bird/Frank Lane Picture Agency 111B; Borrell Casals/Frank Lane Picture Agency 99; Robert Pickett 93BR, 102
Carolyn Fry 80, 174TL, 182–4
GAP Photos: Claire Davies 92BR; FhF Greenmedia 93TL; Tim Gainey 93TR, 111; Geoff Kid 103TL; Zara Napier 113; Juliette Wade 103TR
GPL: Mark Winwood 101T
Getty Images: Hulton Archive 166
Andrew Lawson Photography: 106–7
Lindley Library: 34BR, 35TL, 36, 39, 40, 46, 60, 64, 75, 90BL, 167
Allan Pollok-Morris: 1, 2–3, 4–5, 7, 9, 14, 16–17, 20–21, 23, 34TR, 28–9, 35TR, 35BL, 48–9, 61, 62–3, 64–5, 66–7, 70, 71, 78, 85, 87, 96, 108, 115, 116–17, 119, 128–9, 136, 138, 139, 142TR and BL, 143TR and BL, 148–9, 150, 156, 160–61, 168, 169, 170, 171, 172, 189, 190, 191, 192, 193, 196TR and BR, 202–3, 204, 207, 208, 210, 212, 213, 214, 215, 216, 217, 218–19.
RHS: 10, 29, 44, 92, 101B, 118, 135, 142TL and BR, 143BR, 174TL and B, 175BR, 185, 186, 188, 196TL, 198, 199; Sue Drew 147; Herbarium Dept 110T, 145, 146, 151, 152, 153, 154–5, 159, 162, 163, 165; A. Mitchell 93BL, 101B, 114, 143TL; Stephen Record 19, 22, 133, 173; Tim Sandall 10T, 11TR and BL, 92BL, 120TL and BR, 121TR and BL, 174TR and BL, 175TR and BL; Jane Sebire 73, 88–9, 90–91; Mike Sleigh 10BR, 11TL, 11BR, 13, 25, 26, 27, 32, 34TL, 34BL, 35BR, 53, 56, 58, 59, 64T, 68, 69, 95, 103B, 120TR and BL, 121TL and BR, 140, 141, 158, 196BL, 197, 201; Ian Waghorn 105

This book is published to accompany the BBC television series *A Passion for Plants*, first broadcast on BBC2 in 2007.

Executive producer Jo Vale
Series producers Sally Thompson and Amanda Murray

Published in 2007 by BBC Books in association with the RHS.
BBC Books is an imprint of Ebury Publishing.
A Random House Group Company

1 3 5 7 9 10 8 6 4 2

The Random House Group Limited Reg. No. 954009

Addresses for companies within the Random House Group can be found at www.randomhouse.co.uk

A CIP catalogue record for this book is available from the British Library.

ISBN 978 1 84607239 0

The Random House Group Limited makes every effort to ensure that the papers used in our books are made from trees that have been legally sourced from well-managed and credibly certified forests. Our paper procurement policy can be found at www.randomhouse.co.uk

Commissioning editor Nicky Ross
Project manager Christopher Tinker
Project editor Helen Armitage
Designer Isobel Gillan
Production controller Katherine Hockley

Printed and bound by Firmengruppe APPL, aprinta druck, Wemding, Germany

To buy books by your favourite authors and register for offers visit www.rbooks.co.uk